Pirates and Privateers in the 18th Century

Dedicated to Luca and Maya Human, the twin terrors of the Southern Ocean!

Pirates and Privateers in the 18th Century

The Final Flourish

Mike Rendell

PEN & SWORD
HISTORY

AN IMPRINT OF PEN & SWORD BOOKS LTD.
YORKSHIRE - PHILADELPHIA

First published in Great Britain in 2018 by
Pen & Sword History
An imprint of
Pen & Sword Books Ltd
Yorkshire - Philadelphia

ISBN 978 1 52673 165 4

A CIP catalogue record for this book is available from the British Library.

Typeset by Aura Technology and Software Services, India
Printed and bound in England By TJ International Ltd.

Pen & Sword Books Ltd incorporates the Imprints of Pen & Sword Books
Archaeology, Atlas, Aviation, Battleground, Discovery, Family History, History,
Maritime, Military, Naval, Politics, Railways, Select, Transport, True Crime,
Fiction, Frontline Books, Leo Cooper, Praetorian Press, Seaforth Publishing,
Wharncliffe and White Owl.

For a complete list of Pen & Sword titles please contact
PEN & SWORD BOOKS LIMITED
47 Church Street, Barnsley, South Yorkshire, S70 2AS, England
E-mail: enquiries@pen-and-sword.co.uk
Website: www.pen-and-sword.co.uk

or

PEN AND SWORD BOOKS
1950 Lawrence Rd, Havertown, PA 19083, USA
E-mail: uspen-and-sword@casematepublishers.com
Website: www.penandswordbooks.com

Contents

Preface

Mention the word 'pirate' to most people and they will summon up an image of a swashbuckling buccaneer, shouting in a mock-Cornish accent and using phrases such as 'Heave-ho me hearties' and 'Yo-ho-ho and a bottle of rum!' They will think of the heroic figures from films such as *The Pirates of the Caribbean*. They may bring to mind 'booze cruises' in the Caribbean on board the *Black Pearl* as she sailed into the sunset. They may think of buried treasure and bearded men armed with cutlasses. But what they probably will not think of is theft, rape, murder, arson and torture. Yet, sweeping aside the nostalgia and putting down the rose-tinted spectacles, that was, more often than not, the reality of piracy in the seventeenth and eighteenth centuries.

The period is said to be the Golden Age of Piracy – as if it was something vaguely noble and aspirational. This golden age, lasting from perhaps 1650 to 1730, is divided into three parts – up to 1680; from 1680 to 1710; and from 1710 to 1730. Each period had its own characteristics and the object of this book is to look behind the myths, to consider the importance of piracy and privateering to the British economy, and to see how and why piracy came to be seen as an almost virtuous, anodyne, past-time. It looks, in particular, at the third and final phase of the golden age, while at the same time showing how it differed from its earlier manifestations.

Some of the pirates are household names, whereas some are almost lost to history. And because pirates did not often sit down in the genteel surroundings of the artist's studio, they rarely had their picture painted – at least not in their lifetime. So, in many cases we have little idea of what they actually looked like. There are woodcuts – particularly from a book published in 1724 – but these may or may not bear any resemblance to the men portrayed.

This book is intended to consider pirates and privateers in the context of the era in which they lived, rather than viewing them from a twenty-first-century perspective. They lived their lives in their time, not ours, and we should not rush to judge them by our own standards.

The pirate Edward Teach, a.k.a. Blackbeard.

Part One

Background

A seventeenth century Spanish galleon.

Chapter 1

A General History of the Pyrates

This present book is about pirates and privateers, particularly during the final phase of their 'golden age'. It is, however, important to distinguish between the two groups. Piracy was illegal. It was regarded as a threat to international trade; its practitioners were despised and reviled. Pirates were seen as the scum of the earth, a menace to society. Privateers on the other hand were patriotic sailors serving the interests of their country; hard-working and pursuing a noble cause. In practice, both groups did precisely the same thing – they went to sea in order to capture other vessels, to loot their cargoes and to grow rich on the proceeds of plunder. The only difference between the two groups was that privateering was legal – encouraged by a government which found it convenient to leave private individuals to implement foreign policy without involving the state in expense or responsibility. The distinction between pirate and privateer was that the latter held a Letter of Marque, but even this distinction was blurred, because many privateers exceeded their authority and stepped over into piracy. Other pirates became privateers – at least in their own minds – because they managed to purchase a Letter of Marque corruptly, or simply joined up with other privateers to form a mixed squadron of vessels lying in wait for their prey.

Admiral Horatio Nelson was one person who saw little distinction between the two classes of mariner, writing that 'the conduct of all privateers is, as far as I have seen, so near piracy that I only wonder any civilized nation can allow them'.

Where the distinction between piracy and privateering is unclear, it is easier to use the term 'buccaneer' because it avoids making a distinction. The word comes from the Carib word 'buccan' meaning a wooden frame on which strips of meat would be air-dried. The meat was often eaten by sailors throughout the Caribbean – hence 'buccaneers'. Strictly speaking it does not therefore apply to 'the Brethren' (as pirates sometimes called themselves) in other parts of the world.

It is difficult to escape the conclusion that if the person committing the piratical act was British, it was viewed in Britain in a wholly different light from an act by, say, a Frenchman or a Spaniard. Even more xenophobic, if the victims were Indian, or from one of the countries bordering the Arabian Gulf, then this was seen almost as a just dessert – they were too rich for their own good, and relieving them of their jewels and vast fortunes was in some way 'fair'.

A GENERAL

HISTORY

OF THE

PYRATES,

F R O M

Their firſt RISE and SETTLEMENT in the Iſland of
Providence, to the preſent Time.

With the remarkable Actions and Adventures of the two Female Pyrates

MARY READ and ANNE BONNY;

Contain'd in the following Chapters,

To which is added.

A ſhort ABSTRACT of the Statute and Civil
Law, in Relation to Pyracy.

The ſecond EDITION, with conſiderable ADDITIONS

By Captain CHARLES JOHNSON.

L O N D O N:

Printed for, and ſold by *T. Warner*, at the *Black-Boy* in *Pater-Noſter-Row*, 1724.

Pirates generated a fascinated horror in the eyes of the general public in the eighteenth century. This fascination was fed by one particular book, published in 1724 under the pseudonym of Captain Charles Johnson, and entitled *A General History of the Robberies and Murders of the most notorious Pyrates*. This book, more than any other, fed and inspired the public appetite for stories of piracy and mayhem on the High Seas.

For years it has been assumed that the book was actually the work of Daniel Defoe, who, it is believed, used several hundred aliases during his career. More recently the finger of authorship has been pointed at a Grub Street hack called Nathaniel Mist. Quite possibly one of the reasons why Defoe was assumed to be the author was that he was a 'plant' in Mist's printing offices, put there by the Walpole administration to spy on Mist and to keep an eye on his activities.

Certainly, Mist would have had the contacts in the government – and the knowledge of seamanship - to have assembled this tale of over thirty pirates. In a way the authorship is neither here nor there – the book fitted in with a series of other stories designed to frighten and fascinate. Similar tales about notorious highway robbers, or about sensational murders, gripped the readership of what would later be termed 'penny dreadfuls'. Safe in the security of their own homes, men and women could read about dastardly deeds and swashbuckling buccaneers – and be glad that they were not adrift on the Seven Seas, pursued by black-hearted villains and bearded cut-throats.

The *General History* was a commercial success – and it also became the inspiration for many subsequent authors including Robert Louis Stevenson with *Treasure Island* (1883) and J M Barrie with *Peter Pan* (1911). In its original form, the *General History* was issued in two volumes: the first, covering the most recent period of piracy, gave biographical details of twenty-one pirates; and the second dealt with the earlier exploits of another thirteen pirates, of whom perhaps three were fictitious. Their inclusion obviously casts doubt on the veracity of some of the other stories told about real-life pirates. The author was clearly not going to let the truth get in the way of a good story....

Within two years the book had run to four editions, and these established pirate literature as a sub-genre in its own right. Running to over 300 pages, the *General History* was of course a work of fiction – and many of the facts set out in it are uncorroborated and quite possibly heavily embellished. It does however introduce its readers to one-legged pirates with wooden crutches, and half-blind pirates with eye patches, and puts forward the idea of buried treasure. It painted its tales with gunnels awash with blood, and generally set the tone for the tongue-in-cheek portrayal of pirates in modern day films such as *Pirates of the Caribbean*. The book romanticised the stories, giving the characters a mythical status. The murders, the thieving and the torture became exciting tales of derring-do, designed to terrify, excite and amuse. They were not intended to be truthful – and may even have been inspired by the author's Jacobite anti-establishment views. If the author was indeed Nathaniel Mist, he had once served as a sailor on board a ship operating in the West Indies. He knew the hardships faced by sailors, and had experienced their conditions, eaten their food, survived on their wages.

He later went on to publish his *Weekly Journal* – one of the most outspoken newspapers attacking Sir Robert Walpole's Whig administration, and vilifying the House of Hanover. Small wonder that a man who referred to George I as 'a cruel ill-bred uneducated old Tyrant, and the driveling Fool, his Son' would show law-breakers and anti-establishment figures in a rosy light. Mist was in frequent trouble with the authorities and ended up fleeing to France to escape being imprisoned for committing a libel on the king. Mist's *Weekly Journal* had a readership of perhaps 10,000. If Mist was the author of the *General History* (and he was entered as such in His Majesty's Stationery Office), it would have given him an even wider platform from which to deliver his anti-authoritarian views.

While much of what we know about pirates in the 'golden age' – the period of fifty years leading up to 1730 – comes from the *General History*, it has to be taken with rather more than just a pinch of salt.

In looking at the exploits of three of the earlier pirates (Morgan, Kidd and Avery), it is worth noting that Captain Morgan was not even mentioned in the *General History*. His story, and those of Kidd and Avery, are included in this book to differentiate their exploits from those of their successors, and to put the activities in the period 1710 to 1730 in context. They are also included because all three men blurred the lines between piracy and privateering, whereas the activities of later exponents were much more clear-cut and obvious.

Plunder

It is easy to assume that all pirates plundered 'treasure' – gold and silver bullion, fabulous jewels, exotic merchandise. The reality is far more down-to-earth. Mostly they seized items of a much more prosaic nature. Bullion was no good if what you really needed were medicines to keep your crew alive. And pirates could not just sail into harbour, go to the nearest chandler to obtain new sails, anchors and so on. Therefore they were always keen to use the ships which they seized as a source of 'floating repair materials'. Pirates were often content to seize items for 'domestic' consumption – everything from pots and pans to candles and anchors. Indeed, on one occasion they apparently confined themselves to stealing the hats belonging to the crew of the ship they captured – to replace the ones they had tossed skyward into the sea the day before. Naturally, they valued gold and silver bullion – but much of what they seized was far more ordinary. When the ship belonging to Edward Teach was captured it was found to have on board twenty-five hogsheads of sugar, eleven tierces and 145 bags of cocoa, a barrel of indigo and a bale of cotton. And not one grain of gold. A tierce, being an old word meaning a third, was a unit of measurement for dried goods.

Of course, there were tales of eye-watering amounts of treasure seized from magnificent galleons, but on a daily basis what the pirates captured tended to be simple fishing boats or trading vessels operating between islands, perhaps doing a spot of contraband running. The pirates' reward might be a small amount of money – the profits made by the merchant in exchanging goods needed by settlers, as well as small quantities of local produce such as tobacco, sugar or rum. Pirates needed to eat, they needed to drink, and they needed tobacco, so there would have been few complaints if the monotony of waiting for 'the big one' was broken by giving chase to far simpler fare.

The myth of buried treasure

If stories about pirates are to be believed, they spent their time digging holes in the sand, or hiding treasure in the backs of caves which could only be entered at low-tide at certain times of the year, and which were guarded by rocks which rolled into place and could not be moved without recourse to forgotten languages and ancient spells. It begs the question: why, when all the crew shared in the treasure, would any one of them want to bury his treasure when there was no certainty that he would ever be able to get back to reclaim it? Yes, there was one instance involving Captain Kidd where he deliberately buried some of the looted gold – but that was partly in order to be able to reveal its hiding place in court, in a vain attempt to save his life. On another occasion it is thought that Francis Drake buried some of his looted treasure because he had insufficient pack animals to transport it back to his ship – only to return and discover that the cache had been retrieved by its lawful, i.e. Spanish, owners. There is also a story about a Captain Norman, operating out of the Virgin Islands, squirrelling away his loot in circumstances whereby he was observed from off-shore. By the time Norman returned to collect his buried belongings they had been 'liberated' by person or persons unknown. It was hardly a precedent likely to inspire others to follow his example!

The other reason why burying treasure was an unlikely event was that more often than not the items looted by the pirates were not gold and silver bullion, but perishables – cargoes of cocoa, cotton and spices. You wouldn't bury tobacco or snuff, or hide rolls of silk and damask. You 'fenced' them in the port you went to after capturing the merchant ship – converting the proceeds into cash, and dividing it up between the crew. When bullion was looted it was much more likely that individual crew-members would take charge of their own share, perhaps stitching the gold into their trousers – in the seams, or wherever. This was certainly the case with some of the crew of Henry Avery's ship the *Fancy*. His exploits are described later, but when some of Avery's men were picked up in England long after their piratical voyage had ended, they were identified as pirates by the precious stones sewn into their clothing.

Captured cargoes consisted of a mixed bag of goods, as evidenced by the testimony of Peter Mainwareing, who turned informant at the trial of Stede Bonnet. His sloop, the *Francis*, had previously been seized by Bonnet off Antigua and Mainwareing deposed that the cargo seized consisted of:

> *26 Hogsheads of Rum … (valued at £256/6/8, Barbados Money); twenty five Hogsheads …. of Molasses (valued at £138/13/8 Antigua money); three Barrels of Sugar (valued at £33 Antigua money); two Pockets of Cotton, and two Bags of Indigo (£12); and that out of a small Trunk of this Informer, they took nineteen Pistoles, two Half-Moidores of Gold, fourteen Crowns, and a Silver Watch of seven Guineas Price, and one Pair of Silver Buckle of twenty five Shillings, Boston Money; and one new Cable, of the Value of fifty Pounds Barbados Money.*

Looted cargo such as this was clearly intended to be sold on the black market, not buried. So, where did the idea of buried treasure come from? In part, it is due to the tale of Long John Silver in Robert Louis Stevenson's *Treasure Island*. He made popular the figure of a pirate with a wooden leg, a parrot on his shoulder, and maps with 'X marks the spot'. Piracy as a romantic endeavour has never looked back.

The Pirate's Round

In the 1690s the pirates developed a new area of operations – the Red Sea. By then the Caribbean was becoming so infested with pirates that opportunities for plunder were limited. By sailing from the West Indies, or the eastern seaboard of the North American colonies, the pirates could travel across the Atlantic to Madeira, pass down the coast of Africa (perhaps doing a spot of plundering along the coast and off the Cape Verde Islands) and then round Cape Hope, travel up through the Mozambique Channel, and find a safe anchorage at Île Sainte-Marie off the coast of Mozambique. There they could re-provision and repair their ships and hunt for merchant shipping in the area up towards Yemen, or over towards the French-controlled Réunion Island, or even to the western coast of India. In particular they would lie in wait for the richly laden ships belonging to the Mughal of India, returning from the annual hajj to Mecca.

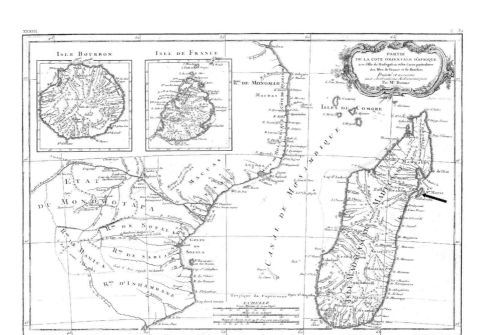

A map of Madagascar dated 1770, with the Île Sainte-Marie arrowed.

Some of the pirates were spectacularly successful – such as Thomas Tew in 1693. He encountered an Indian dhow laden with treasure, and over-ran it without serious opposition. The forty-five crewmen 'liberated' around £100,000, together with merchandise such as ivory, jewels and valuable spices. Each crewman received a minimum of £1,200, with an estimated £8,000 going to Thomas Tew. These were huge sums for sailors who in legitimate employment might be paid £17.50 per annum (peacetime rate) rising to £25 per annum in times of war. There is no doubt that when Tew and his men sailed back across the Atlantic they inspired others to follow in their footsteps. They became known as 'roundsmen' and their piracy was known euphemistically as 'Red Sea trade'.

Madagascar

The island became a separate centre for the pirates, particularly after Port Royal in Jamaica was destroyed by earthquake in 1692 and after the French government cracked down on those pirates who were based on Tortuga, off the coast of modern-day Haiti. Some pirates established communities on land, in particular Abraham Samuel at Port Dauphin, Alan Baldridge on Île Sainte-Marie and James Plantain at Ranter Bay. Stories started to circulate about the pirate Henry Avery when he and his treasure disappeared without trace. The rumour was that he settled on Madagascar and became a local king. The existence of gravestones on the island show that there may have been quite a sizeable population of men linked to piracy who lived and died there, giving rise to talk of a 'pirate utopia' – of a classless, democratic society where men put into place a new order of equality and freedom. There is, however, no evidence whatsoever of this. Johnson's *A General History* went further and suggested that this utopia was a physical place, called Libertalia – a commune made up of freed slaves, pirates and people whose livelihoods were linked to piracy such as chandlers, suppliers and shipwrights. And of course, wherever there are stories about piracy, there are stories that the pirates in question spent their time squirrelling away their ill-gotten gains in secret hiding places. It has to be said that these stories do a great deal for modern day tourism, but may have very little to do with historical accuracy.

What is certainly the case is that any pirate involved in the Pirate Round would have needed provisioning and repairs by the time they reached Madagascar. Île Sainte-Marie, nowadays re-named Nosy Boraha, was the favourite destination and it is highly likely that some criminal elements found that they preferred to stay put, and spend their wealth on drink, gambling and whoring, rather than risk the return journey across the Atlantic, where they might well be recognised, arrested and sent to the gallows. Madagascar provided an easy life, not least because there were no navies patrolling the area, and no effective government.

Torture and Punishment

It was a cruel and sadistic age, and this applied equally to pirate and privateer alike. Some punishments may well be later inventions, such as walking the plank. This was first mentioned in print in Francis Grose's *Dictionary of the Vulgar Tongue*, which was published in 1788:

> *'Walking the plank': A mode of destroying devoted persons or officers in a mutiny on ship-board, by blind-folding them, and obliging them to walk on a plank laid over the ship's side; by this means, as the mutineers suppose, avoiding the penalty of murder.*

Johnson, in his *General History*, refers to a similar practice employed in Roman times, but says that a ladder was used, and that victims were granted freedom if they were able to swim ashore. There are documented instances of pirates forcing captured prisoners to walk the plank in the 1800s, but it was not until 1837 when Charles Ellms used a sensationalist illustration entitled *'A Piratical Scene – Walking the Death Plank'* in his work *The Pirates Own Book* that the punishment caught the public imagination. It was also mentioned on at least three occasions by Robert Louis Stevenson in his 1884 classic *Treasure Island.*

Far worse was keel-hauling, whereby a sailor would be dragged from one side of the ship, under the hull, to the other side. Barnacles could rip the man's skin to pieces. Flogging was also widespread, and the cat o' nine tails, colloquially known as the Captain's Daughter, was used as an instrument of punishment on naval and pirate ships alike. In one very matter-of-fact account of an incident on board the sloop *Revenge*, written in 1745, there is a record of the treatment of a captured negro who, it was believed, had mistreated the crew of an English merchant ship:

> *We then tyed him to a Gun and made the Doctor Come with Instruments Seemingly to Castrate him as they had Served the English, thinking by that means to Gett some Confession out of him, but he still denyed it. We then tyed a Molatto, one that was taken with him, to know if he knew anything about the Matter. We Gave him a dozen of Stripes [i.e. lashes] and he declared that he knew nothing .... However to make Sure and to make him Remember that he bore such a Commission we Gave him 200 Lashes and then pickled him and left him to the Doctor to take Care of his Sore A-se.*

In another instance, in 1704 the captain of the *Rochester* ordered a man to be flogged a truly barbaric 600 times, with a one-inch thick tarred rope. A few years earlier Henry Morgan used horrific torture methods on captives when he overran Panama City, in order to ascertain where treasure had been secreted away. The methods included stringing men up by the genitals, and slowly burning them.

Being marooned on an uninhabited island, intended as a slow, lingering form of death by starvation or dehydration, was used by pirates as a form of punishment for cheating by crew members. And if Johnson is to be believed, one particularly sadistic pirate by the name of Ned Low was not averse to mutilating his victims and even eating their body parts. His preferred form of torture was to bind the captive's hands and fingers with rope and then set fire to the rope until it burned down to the bone. On some occasions he simply set fire to the captured ship with the passengers still on board, and on another he set a group of whalers adrift in a small rowing boat without any water of provisions. He was not just a pirate, he was a psychopath who seemed to relish in the terror which his very name spread. Even his own men described him as 'a maniac and a brute'.

The ill-treatment of civilian crews, both on merchant ships and aboard privateers, was often cited as the main reason why disgruntled men took up piracy. It was an easy option: one pirate by the name of John Archer said this before he was led to the gallows in 1724: 'I could wish that Masters of Vessels would not use their men with such severity, as many of them do, which exposes us to great Temptations.'

Two years later, William Fly made his final confession before being hanged, proclaiming

'I can't change myself. I shan't own myself guilty of murder – our Captain and his Mate used us Barbarously. We poor men can't have justice done us. There is nothing said to our Commanders. Let them never so much abuse us, and use us like Dogs.'

Hangings

The death penalty was used for a wide array of crimes in the eighteenth century, including wrongdoings which nowadays would be considered minor misdemeanours. Certain days – eight per year – were set aside as 'hanging days' and huge crowds would turn out to watch the events. Some criminals became heroic figures in the eyes of the public and tens of thousands would turn out to watch their death. The crowds would be entertained by street singers composing ballads about the occasion; they could buy souvenirs in the form of prints illustrating the man on the gallows; they could within days buy copies of the condemned man's final speech. In the case of the original 'Jack the lad' (in fact a young man called John Shepherd), he was so popular on account of the number of times he had escaped from custody, even when padlocked to the cell floor, that 200,000 people are believed to have gathered to see him off on his final journey in 1720. To put it in perspective, London's population at the time was not more than 1 million, so his death attracted one in five of all residents. Another famous criminal given hero status was the stylish highway robber known as 'Sixteen String Jack' – on account of the coloured ribbons he wore, dangling from his knees. His real name was John Rann and he was hanged (wearing a pea-green suit bought specially for the occasion, and sporting a huge nosegay) at the age of 24 in 1774 before a vast and enthusiastic crowd. The crowd were not disappointed by this flamboyant character – he danced a jig for them and exchanged banter before making his final exit. Pirates attracted a similar cult following, with people both horrified and fascinated by their lifestyle.

A whole range of words grew up to describe hangings. Slang expressions for a hanging included 'a rope dance', 'a trining', or 'a nubbing'. To 'dangle in the sheriff's picture frame' meant the same thing, as did 'stretching'. A hanging day was colloquially known as a 'wry neck day', and the 'chates' was another name for

the gallows. A man who repented on the gallows was said to 'die dunghill'. Another name for the gallows was a 'three-legged mare' or 'Gregorian Tree'. The 'topping cove' was the hangman.

In London, whereas non-piracy criminals were originally hanged at Tyburn, near the site of today's Marble Arch, pirates sentenced by the Admiralty Court had their own rendezvous with death: Execution Docks. Since the fifteenth century these took place within the jurisdiction of the court, at Wapping, just above the low water mark. Here, a specially shortened rope was used, meaning that there was less of a drop. Consequently, the convicted pirate usually died slowly of asphyxiation, resulting in a macabre dance-like struggle known as the Marshal's Dance.

The Admiralty were keen that the pirates should be seen to suffer – theirs was no quick death behind closed doors. A hanging procession would start from the prison at Marshalsea in Southwark early in the morning, wending its way through the streets with the pirate chained and sitting facing backwards in a cart. They would cross London Bridge and enter the City. The procession would be led by the master or senior official of the court, holding aloft a silver paddle, his symbol of power. The procession would generally stop at the Turks Head public house where the condemned man would have his final quart of beer, before trundling over to the site of the Execution Dock in Wapping. Sometimes the prisoners were totally inebriated and out cold by the time they arrived at their rendezvous with the rope. *The Gentleman's Magazine* for January 1796 (v. 66, Pt 1, page 161) states:

> *This morning about ten, Michael Blanch, a Spaniard, James Colley an American, and Francis Cole, a Black, who were found guilty at the late Admiralty Sessions of the wilful murder of William Little, the master and commander of an American vessel, were brought out to Newgate, and placed in a cart, and conveyed to Execution Dock, where they were executed according to their sentence. In the afternoon the bodies were brought back to Surgeon's Hall, there to be dissected pursuant to the sentence of the Court of Admiralty. Had it been a case of piracy they would have been hanged in chains.*

The *European Magazine, and London Review*, reporting on the same execution in its edition of 4 February 1796, stated that Colley 'seemed in a state resembling that of a man stupidly intoxicated, and scarcely awake....'

Traditionally the gallows would be sited so that the man's feet would be touching the water at low tide as he was hanged. After death, his body would be

Thomas Rowlandson's drawing of a crowd observing a multiple hanging scene, date unknown.

left to be covered by the rising tide three times, to symbolically cleanse it, and the body would then be removed from the gallows. In a few cases the body would be buried in an unmarked pauper's grave, but as mentioned in the extract from the *Gentleman's Magazine*, more usually the corpse would be seized and passed on to anatomists for medical research and teaching purposes. A rather more grizzly ending was in store for the more notorious pirates – gibbetting.

Gibbetting

In order to make an example of the fate awaiting pirates the body of the hanged man would sometimes be gibbetted. This involved coating the corpse in tar, to help preserve it. The body would then be placed in a cage with hooped metal bars and hung up alongside the river so that all sailors approaching and leaving the port would have to pass the macabre and malodorous scene. Where groups of pirates were hung, their corpses might be lined on either side of the river where they would slowly decompose. It is hard to imagine the nauseous smell and appalling sight of decomposing corpses, being pecked at by scavenging birds, which greeted the sailors on their journey up and down the Thames. In the case of the notorious Captain Kidd, who was hanged in 1701, his corpse remained on view for several years.

Ethnicity

It is easy to assume that piracy was a white man's profession, and that black Africans played no part. That would be wholly incorrect, and some of the pirate ships were manned by a significant number of former slaves. On many ships between a third and a half of the crew may have fallen into this category – either made up of slaves who had run away and chosen to go to sea, or who had been captured by pirates.

Why might they join the pirates? Because it spared them from being sold back into slavery – because it gave them a chance to make a living, albeit in tough conditions. Some historians speak of this as a truly egalitarian experiment – African slaves and European sailors serving under a single flag, sharing the spoils and with an equal voice. The truth is hard to ascertain but it is by no means certain that the equality extended as far as sharing plunder on a purely *per capita* basis – there are suggestions that former slaves might expect half or even one third of that taken by their white counterparts. And the one-man-one-vote system may have applied to selecting the captain, but not as far as saying, 'Drop me off on the African mainland, I want to go home.' There were very few first mates or captains who had started off as slaves, and it is difficult to escape the conclusion that in many cases they were welcomed on board in order to provide 'grunt' – the muscle needed to haul the ropes, raise and lower the sails, and to man the cannon. Pirate ships needed men to crowd on deck, to wave swords and fire muskets while shouting threats and insults at terrified peace-loving sailors – and small wonder that the pirates were eager to use African former slaves who were more than willing to provide the numbers. In many cases they were ferocious and brave fighters, often the first to board a vessel under attack.

There were a few leadership exceptions: on one occasion a pirate of mixed race only known to history as 'Old South', led the men who sailed aboard one of the many ships called *Good Fortune*. There are also a number of other black and mixed race pirates who flourished in the seventeenth century, but none as famous or as successful as their white counterparts.

'Black Caesar' is often cited as an example of a captured African who became a successful pirate leader – he later served with Edward Teach as lieutenant on board the *Queen Anne's Revenge*. Teach had ordered Caesar to put a lighted fuse to the powder store if the ship was in danger of being captured, but Caesar was prevented from carrying out the order. He did not outlive his captain for long, and met his fate on the gallows in 1718 at Williamsburg, Virginia. Other blacks captured by the authorities were generally sold straight back into slavery and were not actually tried for piracy. Hence one third of the crew captured when Bartholomew Roberts was killed – amounting to seventy men – was sold into slavery. There is no way of knowing how many slaves were actually found guilty of piracy – the records of hangings did not disclose their ethnicity.

Flags

One of the problems facing privateers was that not all ships flew their own flag – and given that the Letter of Marque only applied to ships from a specified country, it was really important that nationality was established correctly. Even Royal Navy ships were not averse to flying the flag of their enemy if they thought that it would give them an advantage, i.e., in approaching a vessel without attracting attention. In 1743 when Admiral George Anson gave chase to the Spanish treasure galleon known as *Nuestra Señora de Covadonga* ('Our Lady of Covadonga') he had no qualms in raising the Spanish flag in the hope that the *Covadonga* would think, from a distance, that she was an escort vessel.

Flags had always been used to communicate intent, and pirates and privateers alike were happy to confuse such intent by flying the 'wrong' flag. Pirates might fly any number of captured flags while they were at sea, but when they attacked they had a choice of two – one red and the other black. The red one was originally known by its French name – the 'Jolie rouge', meaning 'pretty red', corrupted over time to 'Jolly Roger'. This may have happened because 'Old Roger' was also a nick-name for the devil, and therefore 'Jolly Roger' had a particular resonance. It was blood red, generally plain, and meant: 'We are pirates, we are going to board your ship. Resistance is futile because we are going to kill you all – no quarter will be given'.

Sometimes the pirates preferred a more gentlemanly form of declaration of intent, and would fly the plain black flag. That meant a slightly different thing – more akin to when they were privateers. It meant: 'We are pirates, we are going to board your ship. Resistance is futile but if you surrender immediately we will spare everyone on board.' Sometimes this was remarkably effective – running up the black flag would dishearten the enemy so much that they would hand over control without a shot being fired.

On one occasion in 1720 Bartholomew Roberts sailed into a harbour at Newfoundland with a black flag flying. This resulted in the crews of all twenty-two vessels in port panicking and abandoning their ships. Combined, they would have been far too strong for Roberts on his own, but they all fled without a fight once they saw the black flag.

Over time different pirates embellished their own flags, both red and black, with their own emblems. And so we got the skull and crossbones, against a red background, and the skeleton with a spear stabbing a red heart.

Some pirates preferred a figure holding an hour-glass, i.e., showing that the sands of time had run out. Others chose a hand holding a cutlass, and so on. Eventually, the skull and crossbones became identified as an all-purpose pirate flag, and all the flags became known as the Jolly Roger, whatever their colour and whatever the design. In practice, the skull and crossbones may well date back to the Knights

Templar, and to the flags used on their ships in the Mediterranean – as far back as the thirteenth century.

One of the first times it appeared in print was in 1724 as an illustration in *A General History of the Pyrates*, where the pirate Stede Bonnet is shown with a skull and crossbones flag flying from the ship's stern.

Chapter 2

Letters of Marque and Codes of Conduct

The Concise Oxford Dictionary defines Letters of Marque as being a licence to fit out an armed vessel and employ it in the capture of an enemy's merchant shipping. In its singular form, 'letter of marque' could also be used to describe the actual ship carrying the licence.

In its early days a Letter of Marque and Condemnation, to give it its full title, would be granted to an individual who could show that he had suffered loss at the hands of a ship belonging to a foreign power. The licence enabled him to retaliate by seizing goods to an equivalent value from any other ship belonging to that country. This sort of tit-for-tat arrangement was seen as a perfectly normal way of settling international disputes and had been used since the Middle Ages. The person requesting the Letter of Marque would have to specify the nature of his loss, which country had occasioned it and so on. The person being granted the Letter would need to give a bond to ensure that the conditions attached to the Letter were complied with. In particular, the Letter would restrict reprisals to action against shipping from a specified country – and woe betide a merchant who exceeded the authority by not recognising the neutrality of other countries, or who attacked ships belonging to a friendly power. Armed with his Letter the merchant would sail away, and having captured a qualifying vessel would bring it back to Britain so that the Admiralty, or Prize Court, could confirm that the prize was legitimate and then 'condemn' the vessel to be sold and the proceeds paid to the merchant holding the licence.

The important point was that the vessel had to be brought back for adjudication – the privateer could not simply sell it. As Robert Auchmuty, one of the Admiralty Judges stated in 1741:

> *The Sense and Understanding the Law hath of Privateers, viz. That they Are such as receive no pay but go to war at their Own charge, and Instead of pay leave is granted to Keep what they can take from the Enemy, and alth'o such License is Granted yet may they not of their Own heads Convert to their Private use Prizes before the same have Been Adjudged by Law Lawfull to the Captors.*

By the time Elizabeth I came to the throne, England was not strong enough to take on the might of Spain, but the queen was happy enough to use privateers – such as Francis Drake – to pursue national interests. The queen could throw her arms up in horror when the Spanish Ambassador protested at the atrocities carried out by Drake and pretend that it was nothing to do with her – and then happily share the looted gold, silver and other treasure captured and brought back to England. She even knighted Drake for his services – while still maintaining that England was not at war. (It wasn't me, honest, Gov.) We might see it as an unusual foreign policy – but by and large it worked, and Queen Elizabeth and Sir Francis Drake both prospered under the arrangement.

The Letter of Marque would be signed either by the monarch in person or by his/her authorised representative. By the middle of the seventeenth century the Letters were once again being used as an extension of foreign policy. No longer was there any question of loss and compensation. In its place came a device to secure an auxiliary navy, manned by a highly motivated and patriotic crew. It proved extremely popular with the British Government but was also used by all the other naval powers in Europe. In France it was called a *lettre de course* – hence the people operating them were known as 'corsairs'. In Britain the people operating under a Letter of Marque were called privateers – and the same name was also applied to the ship they sailed on.

For the British Government it was a simple decision: supposing you were at war with France or Spain and wanted to build a warship. This meant raising taxation, waiting for some years while the ship was constructed and fitted out, all the time running the risk that the original dispute might finish so that the ship would no longer be needed. A classic example of this was the vessel which was to become Lord Nelson's flagship, HMS *Victory*. She was ordered in 1758, laid down in 1759 and launched in 1765. By then, the Seven Years War was over, and the vessel was no longer required. She was moored up in the River Medway, and slowly left until her keel became home to all manner of marine life. She represented a total waste of the cost of construction – equivalent to more than £7.5 million in today's money. Years passed, and it was not until this white-elephant-of-a-vessel was finally commissioned in 1778, that she started her illustrious career. Two decades of inaction! No wonder the British Government preferred to supplement its navy by getting others to take the risks, to provide the ships, and to be responsible for the payment of the sailors' wages. Even better, the government could call for a share of any plunder recovered by the privateer.

Letters of Marque were used as a way of promoting British colonial interests in the West Indies. Governors of the different islands happily issued letters in the name of the king – and armed with these the privateers would sail off and seize cargoes, attack enemy shipping and in many cases, loot and burn settlements on the mainland and on other islands. In doing so Britain promoted its own economic interests while at the same time harassing and damaging foreign interests, especially Spanish ones. Long before Nelson went with the West Indian fleet to patrol the Caribbean, private ships had filled that role.

The British were by no means alone in using 'private warships' in this way. In the American Revolutionary War the colonies had no navy to speak of – but privateers acting on their behalf seized over 2,000 British merchant vessels and brought them back to the colonial ports where they were adjudged to be prizes of war.

It is also ironic that the very dominance of the Royal Navy over their French counterparts in the 1790s (when French ships were effectively blockaded inside their own harbours, such as at Brest) led to an explosion in French privateering. If the French could not reckon to win the *guerre d'escadre* (in other words a conflict based on conventional fleet warfare), they could still damage British trade interests via a *guerre de course*, using corsairs, i.e., privateers. They did so most successfully, particularly damaging British shipping in the Channel. Operating especially from Saint-Malo and Dunkirk, French privateers threatened to bring merchant shipping to its knees. Based on the Atlantic ports of Nantes and La Rochelle they raided shipping in the Atlantic, and from Toulon and Marseilles they disrupted shipping in the Mediterranean. In the Caribbean, an estimated thirty French ships operated out of Guadaloupe, causing significant damage to the prosperity of the plantation islands. In total, during the period between 1793 and 1800 some 4,314 British merchant ships were captured by the French. To show this in comparison there were around 3,000 ships lost in storms or run aground and wrecked during the same period.

In time the British Navy was able to curtail privateering activities by seizing over a third of the privateering vessels operating out of Saint-Malo. Putting this in context, over the course of the eighteenth century it has been estimated that the British lost a colossal 11,000 ships to privateering raids.

British domination over the French navy meant that British privateers, generally operating out of Bristol, were far less active during the 1790s than they were in earlier wars. Bristol's heyday was in the period of the Seven Year's War, 1756–63, and again in the American Revolutionary War, when between thirty and forty ships each year left Bristol armed with Letters of Marque.

One other theatre of war proved especially fruitful for French privateers in the latter years of the eighteenth century – on the East Indian trade routes. Here, Robert Surcouf was dominant, seizing some forty merchant ships in a fifteen-year period. Some of his captures were remarkable. His schooner the *Émilie* carried four cannon and twenty-six men.

Nevertheless, he overcame the *Triton*, with twenty-six guns and carrying 150 men. Surcouf had managed to take the ship by surprise, approaching the *Triton* while flying a British flag. He then unleashed a fierce assault, killing the captain and all of the officers. A similar success led to the capture of the East Indiaman *Kent*. When accused by a captured British prisoner that he only fought for money, whereas the British fought for honour, Surcouf allegedly replied: 'Each of us fights for the thing we lack most.'

What is remarkable is that all of Surcouf's activities were carried out despite having no Letter of Marque entitling him to seize shipping, merely a *congé de navigation* allowing him to attack in self-defence. Despite this, he was rewarded with the *Légion d'Honneur* and returned to France an extremely wealthy man, dying peacefully in 1829. To the British he had been a pirate; to the French he was a national hero.

Perhaps the most extensive use of Letters of Marque was when America went to war with Great Britain in 1812. The American navy was small – as few as twenty-two ships – but during the war some 538 privateers were hired to harass British interests. Some were American, operating out of Baltimore, while many more were French. They enjoyed an uneven success, with perhaps 300 ships failing to capture any prizes at all. This left a few privateers to do almost all the damage, with the most successful being the *America*, a twenty-gun sloop which captured no fewer than twenty-six British vessels.

Some estimates suggest that ten per cent of British goods intended for use by the armed forces were intercepted in this way – causing increasing problems with over-stretched supply lines. In total, over 2,000 British ships were seized, carrying cargoes worth $40 million at the time. More to the point it discouraged traders from setting out on their journeys and sent insurance premiums soaring. In turn, this led ship owners and merchants to bring pressure on the politicians to find a peaceful solution.

Not that the effectiveness of privateers in the 1812 war was entirely one-sided; it is estimated that British privateers captured some 350 American merchant ships, with another 1,000 seized by the Royal Navy. On Lake Erie it is estimated that American trade dropped by eighty per cent as a direct result of these successes, with insurance premiums rising rapidly until they were a whopping fifty per cent of the value of the cargo being carried.

Meanwhile Canadian privateers successfully harassed American shipping, with an estimated forty privateers operating out of Nova Scotia seizing some 200 American vessels. These successes – and losses – forced changes in the way that the navies of both Britain and America operated. More time was taken up pursuing privateers, and worse, they were forced to operate in pairs in order to make the naval vessels themselves less vulnerable to attack. It may seem odd that privateers were able to attack warships, but it happened, sometimes with great success as with the capture of the 16-gun schooner HMS *Dominica* off the coast of South Carolina in

1813, by the much smaller and lightly armed schooner *Decatur*. In another instance the intrepid *Comet*, sailing off the coast of Brazil, encountered a British naval vessel guarding three merchantmen. The *Comet* successfully outwitted the warship and seized the merchant ships.

The use of Letters of Marque was discontinued by many countries following the signing of the Declaration of Paris in 1856. However, the United States still lacked a large navy at that time and declined to sign until a formal treaty was entered into at the start of the twentieth century. Indeed, under the American constitution the President still has legal powers to issue Letters of Marque, and in the aftermath of the 9/11 attacks (regarded as 'air piracy') there have been suggestions that the Letters of Marque could again be used. Instead of America declaring war on an Arab nation harbouring terrorists, the idea would be that private individuals would be licensed to act on a freelance basis, but with an indemnity from the state for any wrongdoing. In practice, the enabling legislation was not passed, but it perhaps shows that the use of such a device may one day be dusted off and used again against non-state terrorism.

What of the ships used by the privateers? Sometimes they were ordinary merchant ships, but over time the privateers preferred to use ships built with speed in mind – speed to catch up with their prey, speed to escape capture from any naval patrols. By the early 1700s some of the fastest ships afloat were privateers, most of them armed with six- and twelve-pound guns. They were heavily manned, so that the crew could mount effective attacks on other shipping and also to engage in shore skirmishes, and to ensure that there were sufficient crew to man any ships taken as prizes. In theory at any rate, all sailors on board a privateer were granted protection under the rules of war – in practice, of course, any English sailor caught by the Spanish was likely to be hanged without trial – or end up in a Spanish prison in unbelievably appalling conditions. The same was also true in reverse, since many of the English privateers, such as Captain Morgan, were content to resort to torture to find out where treasure had been hidden.

Who would be attracted to the life of a privateer? The answer is that it was seen as a patriotic, and even noble, calling, serving one's country and experiencing the chance of making a considerable fortune. Unlike sailors in the navy who were paid a wage at the end of the voyage, a sailor on a privateering ship had no guarantee of any wage whatsoever. Instead he had a chance to share in any plundered goods and in any prize money awarded by the Prize Courts. This made the sailors highly motivated – and all took advantage of one particular feature of life on board – the privateers code.

The code – more accurately 'Articles of Agreement', or 'Codes of Conduct' – developed out of *Charte-Partie*, a legal document used by privateers in the late seventeenth century. These charters, often administered by the courts in Jamaica where they were known as the 'Jamaica Discipline', were used to prevent and settle disagreements. They were designed to set out the terms of service, to specify levels of compensation in the event of injury and loss of limb, and to divide up any looted treasure in pre-determined shares. These privateering articles had their origins in the Middle Ages when there was a system of 'joint hands' agreements. These would typically set out how profits from a voyage were to be shared out between the merchant, the ship owner and the crew. One such set of articles, handwritten in 1814, is held by the Smithsonian National Museum of American History. It related to the *Prince de Neuchatel*, one of the most successful privateering ships used by the United States in the war against Britain in 1812. In her short career she captured no fewer than nine British ships in the English Channel, and in 1813 was involved in a firefight with a far larger frigate. When the British eventually captured her, she was brought back to England so that her design could be copied, since she was considered faster than any other vessel of her size.

Under the terms of the Articles it was the owners' responsibility to pay for arming and provisioning the vessel. The owners were to receive half of the proceeds from any vessels seized, and the other half was to be divided among the crew according to rank. As an incentive to brave crewmen, the first two sailors to board an enemy ship were to be awarded six extra shares, and any sailor losing a limb in action received double.

Privateers' codes were somewhat different to the pirate codes. The latter were far more democratic – each pirate had the same vote regardless of rank, age or nationality. In theory, pirates could out-vote who was to be first mate, or navigator, and so on. An example is the occasion when the crew of *Revenge* decided that they had had enough of Stede Bonnet as captain, and sent him packing back to Blackbeard, whose protégé he was. Only during an actual engagement was the captain above democratic control – at any other time he could be demoted, and was then usually allowed to leave, with any loyal supporters, in a smaller craft.

The pirates all shared any plunder on an equal basis – except that the Captain was usually granted a double share, while the first mate and carpenter might have slightly more than a single share. It provided for an interesting democracy on board – at a time when cruelty and injustice were commonplace. But the pirate codes had one other difference to the privateer's code – the latter could be enforced in a Court of Law, whereas the pirates' code could not. Pirates therefore specified their own punishment for breach of the rules. This frequently involved being marooned, or, for lesser infringements, having the ears and nose slit.

It is widely assumed that each pirate was required to sign up to the code – often by making his mark, i.e., with a cross, since most sailors at the time were illiterate.

Other customs supposedly developed whereby the code would be adopted by signing on the head of an axe, or while sitting astride a cannon. It is, however, hard to believe that the code held the status of 'the Holy Grail' as suggested in many modern portrayals.

The privateers' code, unlike the pirate code, was unlikely to provide for anything like an equal distribution of prize money. But for pirates and privateers alike it meant that the crew had a vested interest in capturing as many profitable prizes as possible – and mutinies were common if the crew felt that the captain was not being diligent in pursuing a prize. This was especially true of the 'poor' Captain Kidd, mentioned later. He only captured a handful of ships in his entire career, and was forced by his crew into apprehending a vessel not covered by his Letter of Marque. He was therefore adjudged to have acted as a pirate, not as a privateer, and ultimately paid the price with his life.

A lot has been made of the pirate code in films such as the *Pirates of the Caribbean* franchise. In practice, the code varied from captain to captain, and even from voyage to voyage. It would also be unwise to think that all voyages involved sailors who had all signed up to the code. Many of the crews on board the pirate ships were originally serving on board captured merchantmen – they were offered the chance to live, on condition that they joined the fraternity. They had no choice, no negotiating platform: they either agreed to the existing arrangements, or they were killed. This is supported by the testimony of William Phillips, on trial for piracy in 1722 after the Battle of Cape Lopez. He pleaded, as did many of the other 200 pirates on trial at Cape Coast Castle, that he was forced to sign the pirates' articles, which were offered to him on a dish. Alongside the copy of the articles on the dish had been a loaded pistol … but the court was having none of it, and off he went to the gallows.

In cases where the captured sailor was especially useful to the pirates – such as a surgeon or a skilled carpenter – he might be pressed to stay with the pirates even though no attempt was made to sign the articles. Others, holding less valuable skills, may well have been threatened or tortured until they signed – or plied with alcohol until they had no legal capacity to sign anything at all.

Much has been written about the democratic nature of the codes, as if they formed a deliberate attempt to create a model of society which departed from the prevailing hierarchy of monarchs, nobles, squires and peasants. That rather seems to exaggerate the arrangements; here were sailors carrying out criminal acts, in circumstances where each and every one of them was putting his life on the line if he was captured. They took the same risk, i.e., with their life, so it was not unreasonable they expected an equal say in how that risk should be taken. They did not plan an egalitarian utopia, and they certainly did not create one.

Besides, this 'all for one and one for all' ethos was somewhat undermined by the occasions when booty was very deliberately *not* shared equally, where crew members were cast adrift or marooned so that their share could be awarded elsewhere. An example of this was that when Blackbeard successfully raided Charles Town (now Charleston, in South Carolina) he marooned seventeen members of his crew simply in order to increase his share of the plunder.

The codes covered similar subjects but with interesting differences, The one used by the notorious pirate Bartholomew 'Black Bart' Roberts on board the *Royal Fortune*, in 1722 contained the following rules:

1. Equal rights – equal votes

Every man shall have an equal vote in affairs of moment. He shall have an equal title to the fresh provisions or strong liquors at any time seized, and shall use them at pleasure unless a scarcity makes it necessary for the common good that a retrenchment may be voted.

2. No with-holding of treasure, or theft from other crew members

Every man shall be called fairly in turn by the list on board of prizes, because over and above their proper share, they are allowed a shift of clothes. But if they defraud the company to the value of even one dollar in plate, jewels, or money, they shall be marooned. If any man rob another, he shall have his nose and ears slit, and be put ashore where he shall be sure to encounter hardships.

3. No Gambling

None shall game for money, either with dice or cards.

4. Observe the Curfew

The lights and candles shall be put out at eight at night, and if any of the crew desire to drink after that hour they shall sit upon the open deck without lights.

5. Always be prepared for action

Each man shall keep his piece, cutlass and pistols, at all times clean and ready for action.

6. No women to be allowed on board

No boy or woman [shall] be allowed amongst them. If any man shall be found seducing one of the latter sex and carrying her to sea in disguise, he shall suffer death.

7. All for one, one for all

He that shall desert the ship or his quarters in the time of battle shall be punished by death or marooning.

8. Disputes Resolution

None shall strike another on board the ship, but every man's quarrel shall be ended onshore by sword or pistol in this manner: at the word of command from the Quartermaster, each man being previously placed back to back, shall turn and fire immediately. If any man do not, the Quartermaster shall knock the piece out of his hand. If both miss their aim, they shall take to their cutlasses, and he that draws first blood shall be declared the victor.

9. Compensation for injury

Every man who shall become a cripple or lose a limb in the service shall have eight hundred pieces of eight from the common stock, and for lesser hurts proportionately.

10. Differential shares for the captain and specified ranks

The Captain and the Quartermaster shall each receive two shares of a prize, the Master Gunner and Boatswain, one and one half shares, all other officers one and one quarter, and private gentlemen of fortune one share each.

11. Musicians

The musicians shall have rest on the Sabbath Day only, by right, on all other days, by favour only.

Other codes specified that crew were to remain sober and ready to defend the ship in case of attack – a ludicrous requirement since alcohol seemed to permeate almost all pirate activities at all times. The code used by Captain John Phillips, captain of the *Revenge*, in 1724 stated:

1. *Every Man Shall obey civil Command; the Captain shall have one full Share and a half of all Prizes; the Master, Carpenter, Boatswain and Gunner shall have one Share and quarter.*

2. *If any Man shall offer to run away, or keep any Secret from the Company, he shall be marooned with one Bottle of Powder, one Bottle of Water, one small Arm, and Shot. [In other words, he would be left with a single shot so that he could kill himself].*

3. *If any Man shall steal any Thing in the Company, or game, to the Value of a Piece of Eight, he shall be marooned or shot.*

4. *If any time we shall meet another Marooner that Man shall sign his Articles without the Consent of our Company, shall suffer such Punishment as the Captain and Company shall think fit.*

5. *That Man that shall strike another whilst these Articles are in force, shall receive Moses's Law (that is, 40 Stripes lacking one) on the bare Back.*

6. *That Man that shall snap his Arms, [i.e. use his flintlock] or smoke Tobacco in the Hold, without a Cap to his Pipe, or carry a Candle lighted without a Lanthorn, shall suffer the same Punishment as in the former Article.*

7. *That Man shall not keep his Arms clean, fit for an Engagement, or neglect his Business, shall be cut off from his Share, and suffer such other Punishment as the Captain and the Company shall think fit.*

8. *If any Man shall lose a Joint in time of an Engagement, shall have 400 Pieces of Eight ; if a Limb, 800.*

9. *If at any time you meet with a prudent Woman, that Man that offers to meddle with her, without her Consent, shall suffer present Death.*

This can be compared with the code adopted by both Edward Low and George Lowther, and which was set out in the Boston News-Letter in August 1723:

1. *The Captain is to have two full Shares; the [quarter] Master is to have one Share and one Half; The Doctor, Mate, Gunner and Boatswain, one Share and one Quarter.*

2. *He that shall be found guilty of taking up any Unlawful Weapon on Board the Privateer or any other prize by us taken, so as to Strike or Abuse one another in any regard, shall suffer what Punishment the Captain and the Majority of the Company shall see fit.*

3. *He that shall be found Guilty of Cowardice in the time of engagements, shall suffer what Punishment the Captain and the Majority of the Company shall think fit.*

4. *If any Gold, Jewels, Silver, &c. be found on Board of any Prize or Prizes to the value of a Piece of Eight, & the finder do not deliver it to the Quarter Master in the space of 24 hours he shall suffer what Punishment the Captain and the Majority of the Company shall think fit.*

5. *He that is found Guilty of Gaming, or Defrauding one another to the value of a Royal of Plate, shall suffer what Punishment the Captain and the Majority of the Company shall think fit.*

6. *He that shall have the Misfortune to lose a Limb in time of Engagement, shall have the Sum of Six hundred pieces of Eight, and remain aboard as long as he shall think fit.*

7. *Good Quarters to be given when Craved.*

8. *He that sees a Sail first, shall have the best Pistol or Small Arm aboard of her.*

9. *He that shall be guilty of Drunkenness in time of Engagement shall suffer what Punishment the Captain and Majority of the Company shall think fit.*

10. *No snapping of Guns in the Hold. [A reminder that fire was always considered a major risk on board].*

Reading the codes, with their 'lights out, no booze, no gambling' provisions make the pirates lives seem like a party on the vicarage lawn; it was simply not like that. The rules may have been there as a back-up, and in cases formed the cornerstone of pirate day-to-day life, but it does not mean that pirates lived the life of total abstainers. This is borne out by the frequent occasions when pirate ships were overcome by bounty hunters and by naval forces and where the men were found to be in a state of incoherent, insensate inebriation. This was true with Calico Jack, mentioned later, and also with the capture of both Blackbeard and Bartholomew Roberts. In each case the capture was aided by the fact that the crews had been drinking heavily and were unfit for action. Roberts's crew had been in particularly bad shape, his captor remarking that 'The greatest part of his men were drunk, passively courageous, unfit for Service.'

The prohibition on allowing women on board was commonplace – sailors had traditionally regarded it as bringing bad luck. Not that it stopped Captain Vane, one of the most dangerous of the pirates, from failing to release two woman who had been captured. As Johnson in his *General History* remarked, they were kept by the crew 'for their own Entertainment'. There is also the often-quoted but somewhat over-exaggerated story of the two female pirates, Anne Bonny and Mary Read, recounted in chapter 11.

Why did men become pirates? For some there was little choice – they were captured by pirates and chose to join their captors rather than be killed. For others, it was because they were fed up with the discipline and poor pay and conditions on board the merchant ships they originally signed up on. This is supported by the supposed quote which is attributed to Bartholomew Roberts by Johnson in *A General History of Pyrates*:

> *In an honest service there is thin commons, low wages, and hard labour; in this, plenty and satiety, pleasure and ease, liberty and power; and who would not balance creditor on this side, when all the hazard that is run for it, at worst is only a sour look or two at choking. No, a merry life and a short one shall be my motto.*

An interesting observation was made by Captain William Snelgrave when he was captured by pirates off Sierra Leone in 1719. He had operated slaving ships in the area for thirty years, and was generally well-liked by his crew. He described how one of his captors claimed that 'their reasons for going a–pirating were to revenge themselves on base merchants and cruel commanders of ships'. Only the vociferous support of his crew spared the captain, and he went on to describe his experiences in a book entitled *A New Account of Some Parts of Guinea and the Slave-Trade*, published in 1734. What appears to have shocked the captain most of all was the constant swearing and dreadful language of the pirates, or, as he put it:

> *The execrable oaths and blasphemies I heard among the ships company shocked me to such a degree that in Hell itself I thought there could not be worse; for though many seafaring men are given to swearing and taking God's name in vain, yet I could not have imagined human nature could ever so far degenerate as to talk in the manner those abandoned wretches did.*

For many of the crew on pirate ships gambling was an obsession, notwithstanding the code. The account of Alexandre Exquemelin, who served as a ship's surgeon with men like Henry Morgan, mentions how a fortune of over a quarter of a million 'pieces of eight', shared out by the Captain L'Ollonais, was frittered away in a little over three weeks, with the crew 'having spent it all in things of little value, or at play either of cards or dice.' In the mind of Exquemelin, gambling, swearing, drinking, and frequenting brothels went hand-in-hand. As he remarked:

They are busy dicing, whoring and drinking so long as they have anything to spend. Some of them get through a good two or three thousand pieces of eight in a day – and next day do not have a shirt to their back.

Another observer of life on board a pirate ship was Philip Ashton. Writing in 1722 he commented on the 'vile crew of miscreants' with the words:

it was a sport to do mischief, where prodigious drinking, monstrous cursing and swearing, hideous blasphemies, and open defiance of Heaven, and contempt of hell itself, was the constant employment, unless when sleep somewhat abated the noise and revellings.

This does not suggest that worrying about the code of conduct was paramount in the thoughts of the pirates. Perhaps we can take it that in this respect, though not perhaps in any other, the first film in the *Pirates of the Caribbean* series *(The Curse of the Black Pearl)* got it right when Captain Hector Barbossa, played by Geoffrey Rush, utters the famous line about the Code: 'They're more what you'd call "guidelines" than actual rules.'

Becoming a pirate meant sharing in any prize taken – not some miserly share such as would be awarded to ordinary seamen paid a miserable wage on a merchant ship, but a full equal share which could sometimes be like hitting the jackpot. Of course, not many hit that jackpot, but when they did the result was truly spectacular, as with Henry Avery. He and his men were believed to have sailed off with treasure and valuables worth between £250,000 and £400,000, all to be shared equally. When the Spanish ship *San Pedro* was captured off the coast of Chile in 1681 by Captain Bartholomew Sharp, a member of his crew by the name of Basil Ringrose noted: 'We shared our plunder among ourselves … Our dividend amounted to the sum of 234 pieces of eight to each man'.

Conversely, if the captured vessel was carrying salted fish, or low value goods as opposed to bullion, the share could be somewhat dismal. In this context it is worth noting that when Edward Teach, better known as Blackbeard, was captured in 1718 the value of goods found on board was a startlingly small £2,500. If this was to be shared by all on board it represented a somewhat meagre return for one of the most famous pirates of them all. Far more impressive was Samuel Bellamy. The recovery of just some of the treasure found on board his ship the *Whydah* is described in Chapter 9. Suffice to say that the treasure runs into many thousands of pieces of eight, seventeen gold bars, a number of gold nuggets, a quantity of gold dust, gold necklaces and ornaments, and indeed enough to have made each and every man who had been on board a millionaire.

Theirs was no 'alternative society' or pirate utopia. It has been referred to as the 'commonwealth of pirates' – particularly in relation to New Providence Island in the Bahamas – but the reality was that life for the marauding bunch of criminals and murderers was somewhat harsh and undisciplined. Not that harsh living conditions were anything new to the pirates, most of whom had served in the merchant fleets of one nation or another. As Dr Samuel Johnson said when considering life on board:

No man will be a sailor who has contrivance enough to get himself into jail; for being in a ship is being in a jail with the chance of being drowned.

On another occasion, he contrasted the life of a sailor with that of a prisoner, claiming:

A man in a jail has more room, better food, and commonly better company.

These comments applied equally to both pirates and privateers. In general, there was often very little difference between being a privateer and being a pirate: they did the same things, they pillaged, they stole and they killed. Privateers may have had more discipline, fewer periods of shore-based inactivity and fewer opportunities for drunkenness and gambling, but their on-board living conditions and daily activities were much the same as the pirates they despised. But whereas one activity was regarded as evil, a crime against mankind, and an abomination, the other was seen as a patriotic and fully justified activity. The difference? A piece of paper, signed by or on behalf of the Crown.

So, what went into the piece of paper? What did the Letter of Marque say? One example is the Letter of Marque granted to Captain Henry Morgan in 1670 by Sir Thomas Modyford, the Governor of Jamaica, authorising the good captain to lay waste the Cuban city of St Jago de Cuba. In practice Captain Morgan went off and sacked Panama City. More of his exploits appear in the following chapter of this book, but the text of the letter, complete with flowery legalese and squarely laying the blame on the perfidious Spanish, is set out in Appendix 1.

Various points emerge from the letter giving Morgan his authority: the Governor feared that the Spanish would mount an invasion of Jamaica from their base in Cuba; Morgan was expressly instructed to damage Spanish interests in order to prevent such an occasion arising; it was not enough to capture a few prisoners or loot a couple of merchant ships; and although no mention was made of sacking Panama City it was quite clear that Captain Morgan could go off and do his patriotic duty as he deemed fit. Under the cloak of an official blessing, he did just that.

Chapter 3

The Earlier Years of the Golden Age

Looking at three of the seventeenth-century pirates in turn gives us three very different lives, with three very different outcomes. All blurred the lines between pirate and privateer; all either exceeded their Letter of Marque or never had one. Dealing first with a man who was a brilliant strategist and soldier, a consummate politician and a master of plundering the Spanish Main – Captain Henry Morgan, whose Letter of Marque has just been outlined.

Captain Morgan – otherwise Admiral Sir Henry Morgan

Henry Morgan is believed to have been born in South Wales in around 1635, quite possibly in either Abergavenny or in Llanrumney (near Cardiff). It is not known

Captain Morgan surveying the ruins of captured Panama City.

how or when he made his way to the West Indies, or how he began his career as a privateer. What is known is that in his early twenties he took part in a number of raids on Spanish settlements before setting up his base in Jamaica. This strategically important island had been settled in the 1650s, with settlers encouraged to move there by an offer of 30 acres of land, free. Here his uncle, Edward Morgan, had been appointed lieutenant-governor by Charles II after the restoration of the monarchy in 1660. Henry went on to marry his uncle's daughter, Mary Elizabeth.

England's problem was that she had no navy to defend the settlers, and therefore was willing to grant Letters of Marque to men like Morgan, so that they could defend the island and grow England's power and influence in an area previously dominated by Spain. Morgan became a captain operating in a squadron of buccaneering ships under the overall command of Christopher Myngs and was involved in the sacking of various cities including Santiago de Cuba and Campeche, in Mexico. Campeche had been heavily fortified and after the battle fourteen Spanish ships were seized as prizes, making Morgan a rich young man. Subsequently he helped loot the provincial capital of Villahermosa.

He became a close friend of Sir Thomas Modyford, the Governor of Jamaica, and when diplomatic relations between England and Spain worsened in 1667, Modyford gave Morgan a Letter of Marque which was limited to attacking other ships and expressly prohibited any attacks against permanent settlements, whether on the mainland or on any of the islands. Undeterred by this limitation, in the following year Morgan led a force of 500 men on ten ships which captured and looted the Cuban city of Puerto Principe. He then set his sights on Porto Bello (now in modern-day Panama). The city was the third largest and strongest on the Spanish Main, and on one of the main trade routes between the Spanish territories and Spain. Because of the value of the goods passing through its port, Porto Bello was protected by two castles in the harbour and with a third heavily fortified castle in the town itself.

In July 1668 Morgan anchored up a few miles short of the town, and transferred his men to twenty-three canoes, which they paddled through the night, arriving unseen beneath the castles just before dawn. They captured the three castles and the town quickly surrendered.

These canoes, based upon dug-outs used by Carib Indians, were commonly used by pirates. They were known as periagoes, or pirogues, and typically were rowed with single-ended paddles. Some were fitted with keels, enabling them to carry small sails, but all had a very shallow draft. The larger ones were up to a 80 ft long – ideal for carrying a number of armed men as well as having room to carry off high-value cargo. The shallow draft was crucial for pirates lying in wait in mangrove swamps, waiting for ships to come into view. They could be rowed rapidly into position, and then disappear back into the undergrowth where the merchant ships were unable to give chase. For that reason, many pirates started off with pirogues, graduating to sailing ships once they had successfully seized their prey.

Morgan had lost just eighteen men in the attack on Porto Bello, with a further thirty-two wounded. He stayed for a month, amid allegations of torture, widespread rape and the brutal treatment of prisoners, before returning to Jamaica with over £100,000 in ransom money and booty – perhaps equivalent to £10 million nowadays. Five per cent of that – equivalent to half a million pounds – went into the pockets of Captain Morgan, and twice that amount was paid to the Governor of Jamaica as a bribe for overlooking the limitations on the Letter of Marque. Morgan invested some of his money in acquiring an interest in two plantations on the island.

Morgan did not stay long in Port Royal; in October 1668 he sailed from Jamaica with ten ships and 800 men in an attempt to attack Cartagena, but his plans had to be revised when his flagship *Oxford* caught fire and blew up, killing nearly 300 men. Morgan thereupon elected to try and emulate the successes of the Frenchman François l'Olonnais who, two years earlier, had sacked Maracaibo and San Antonio de Gibraltar on the Venezuelan coast.

In the intervening period the Spanish had increased the fortifications considerably at the narrow entrance of the bay. Once more Morgan used pirogues to land men unseen by the defenders, sacked the fort, captured Maracaibo and in an exact repeat of the exploits of l'Olonnais, 'persuaded' the residents to hand over their wealth. Having sacked nearby San Antonio, Morgan headed back, only to find that the Spanish had re-manned the fortress and had positioned three men o'war across the entrance to the bay. Morgan was bottled in.

He declined to surrender and on 1 May 1669 he ordered his men to dress up a captured vessel to make it look as though it was bristling with guns – in fact they were logs. More logs were cut to length, stood upright on deck and dressed in bandanas to look as though the deck was packed with troops. In fact she was a fire ship, and when she was cut loose and set ablaze she caused havoc in the Spanish fleet. The Spanish flagship *Magdelen* caught fire and sank. The *Santa Louisa* managed to escape and the *Marquesa* was captured. However, even though these three Spanish warships had been put out of action, the defenders in the fort were still in a position to destroy Morgan's ships if they tried to pass.

The Spanish tried to extract a ransom – Morgan retaliated by sending a deputation back to Maracaibo and making it clear he would raze the city to the ground, and kill everyone in it, unless he was given free passage – as well as being paid a ransom reward. It worked. For good measure Morgan feigned a night attack on the fort and under cover of darkness slipped past it on the tide, without unfurling any of the sails. Come the dawn they had passed the fort, with its cannon all facing the wrong way and there was nothing that the Spaniards could do to prevent the escape.

Morgan finally returned to Jamaica with a quarter of a million pesos in treasure and a large quantity of cattle, slaves and merchandise, and was able to buy himself a third plantation.

In 1669 Morgan set his eyes on capturing the major city of Panama, the richest settlement on the entire Spanish Main. Morgan assembled a fleet of thirty-seven ships and an army of 2,000 men. Once more he evaded the Spanish lookouts by using pirogues. The city of Panama was on the Pacific coast, meaning that his forces had to march across the narrow isthmus of Panama. The land journey was extremely arduous and many of the men were near starvation by the time they reached their objective, having been reduced to eating leather hides because of the complete lack of food. When Morgan approached the city the Spanish troops were ill-disciplined and were no match for him. Morgan had split his forces into two groups, with one group hidden from view ready to launch a surprise attack on the Spanish forces when they advanced.

There is a story that the Spanish commander thought it might help spread panic among the attackers if he let loose two large herds of stampeding cattle onto the battlefield. Unfortunately, the cattle panicked, turned around, and trampled the Spanish defenders. The Spanish suffered around 500 casualties against the loss of fifteen of Morgan's men. It was a total rout.

What is not clear is whether Morgan burnt the city to the ground, or whether this was done deliberately by the retreating Spanish in order to prevent anything of value coming into Morgan's possession. He still stayed for several weeks and took away a treasure of some 400,000 pesos. Morgan's problems started when he returned to Jamaica, bringing with him 175 mules and ox carts containing bullion and other valuables, only to find that the Spanish were no longer at war with Britain. One of the terms of the peace settlement was that all Letters of Marque were revoked.

This technically pre-dated the sacking of Panama, and the Spanish authorities were furious. In a major diplomatic incident, Governor Modyford was recalled and spent the next two years locked up in the Tower of London. The British were forced to demand that Morgan return to London to face trial. He arrived in April 1672 to a hero's welcome – to the British public he was seen as having picked up the mantle of Sir Francis Drake. Stories of torture were dismissed as sour grapes – and when Alexandre Exquemelin's book came out, via two different publishers, both of them containing allegations of torture – Morgan sued them both for libel – and won £200 in damages.

There was no question of Morgan being convicted for piracy as he was able to argue that he had acted in good faith and had no way of knowing that peace had been declared. Morgan was knighted by Charles II and sent back to Jamaica with express orders to eradicate piracy. Morgan had other ideas – he got on well with the privateers and pirates infesting Port Royal in Jamaica, at that stage the epicentre of all such activities. He allowed the pirates safe passage in return for being paid a commission based on the value of their cargoes. Morgan could not grant Letters of Marque – but he knew a man who could (the French Governor of Tortuga) and he operated a profitable scam whereby he in effect sold the letters to anyone who wanted them and was prepared to pay. At the age of 45 Morgan was at the pinnacle of his success – he was Vice-Governor of Jamaica, he was a vice-admiral, and he was commandant of the Port Royal Regiment. He used his position to strengthen the island's defences against the threat of Spanish aggression. As a judge of the Admiralty Court, and a Justice of the Peace he had status – and he had enormous wealth thanks to his plantation interests and to the profits from plunder.

Morgan died on 25 August 1688; he was awarded a state funeral, and an amnesty was declared so that pirates and privateers could pay their respects without fear of arrest. He was buried in Port Royal, followed by a 22-gun salute from the ships moored in the harbour. Ironically, when a huge earthquake ripped through Port Royal in 1792, just four years after Morgan's death, two thirds of the entire city disappeared into the sea, along with the cemetery where Morgan was buried.

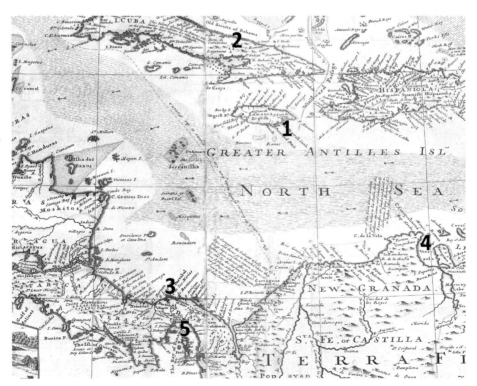

Map extract showing: **1)** Port Royal, Jamaica; **2)** Puerto Principe, Cuba; **3)** Porto Bello; **4)** Maracaibo; **5)** Panama City.

To the extent that he exceeded the terms of the various Letters of Marque awarded to him, Morgan was a pirate, not a privateer. He showed great cruelty as well as courage, and his success transformed Britain's position in the Caribbean. In the century which followed his death the huge riches from the Jamaican plantations flowed back into Britain, providing the investment needed to transform Britain into the world's first industrial super-power. Were it not for Morgan, that wealth and influence would have gone to Spain. For that reason, Morgan was arguably the most important buccaneer of the seventeenth century.

***

Captain Kidd

William Kidd was born in Dundee in 1654. Little is known about his early life, but by 1689 he was serving on a pirate ship off Nevis in the Caribbean. He led a mutiny, took over the ship, renamed it the *Blessed William* and reportedly received a commission from the Governor of Nevis to stay and to harass French shipping in the area – and to defend the island in case of attack. To that extent his activities were those of a privateer, not a pirate, since he was acting on express instructions from the representative of the British Crown.

The Governor informed Kidd and his men that their pay was whatever they could steal from the French. So, Kidd and his crew attacked the French island of Marie Galante and in the process destroyed the town and looted around £2,000. Next, Kidd captured an enemy privateer off the coast of New England and was awarded £150 for his efforts.

However, a year later, Kidd was himself robbed – by a pirate called Captain Robert Culliford, who stole Kidd's ship while he was on Antigua. So much for there being honour among thieves!

The next thing heard of Kidd was that he had moved up to New York – and on 16 May 1691 married one of the wealthiest women in the entire province. His bride, Sarah Bradley Cox Oort, was still in her twenties but had been twice widowed and was a real catch, largely thanks to the fortune left her by her first husband. Kidd helped build Trinity Church but, having settled down for a couple of years, the lure of the sea got too strong.

By then the corrupt Governor Benjamin Fletcher had been replaced by Richard Coote, 1st Earl of Bellomont. In December 1695 the Earl asked the 'trusty and well beloved Captain Kidd' to lead a campaign to capture or kill the notorious pirate Thomas Tew, and 'all others who associated themselves with piracy', and to seize any French ships he came across.

Four-fifths of the cost for the venture was paid for by some of the most powerful men in England: the Earl of Orford, the Baron of Romney, the Duke of Shrewsbury, and Sir John Somers.

A formal Letter of Marque was issued, giving authority 'to Capt. Robert Kidd, commander of the Adventure Galley with a crue of 80 men and mounting 30 guns…'.

The Letter contains a Grant to:

> the said Robert Kidd (to whom our commissioners for exercising the Office of Lord High Admiral of England have granted a commission as a private man-of-war, bearing date 11th day of December 1695) and unto the commander of the said ship for the time being, and unto the officers mariners and others which shall be under your command full power and authority to apprehend seize and take into your custody the said Capt Thomas Too, John Ireland, Capt. Thomas Wake and Capt. Wlm Maze or Mace, as all such pirates, free-booters and sea-rovers, being either our subjects or of other nations associated with them which you shall meet with upon the seas or coasts, with all their ships and vessels, and all such merchandizes, money, goods and wares as shall be found on board, or with them, in case they shall willingly yield themselves, but if they will not yield without fighting, then you are by force to compel them to yield. And we also require you to bring, or cause to be brought, such pirates, free-booters and sea-rovers as you shall seize, to a legal trial to the end they may be proceeded against according to the law in such cases.

All subjects were urged to cooperate with the captain, and he was to keep a detailed journal of all proceedings along with a list of all pirates, vessels and goods captured along the way. The authorisation was given at Kensington on 26 January 1695 and was sealed by King William III. The basis of the authorisation was that the Crown received ten per cent of any plunder and prize money, so at that stage it has to be said that Kidd was acting entirely lawfully. Whatever his preceding pirate activities, Kidd was now legitimate and his powers were wide-ranging.

Kidd sailed across the Atlantic to pick up his new pirate-chasing ship, the *Adventure Galley,* with its handpicked crew. The story goes that as the *Adventure Galley* was sailing down the Thames she passed a naval sloop and for some reason, failed to salute as she passed. Outraged, the sloop fired a shot across her bows – and Kidd's men responded by dropping their trousers and mooning the captain of the sloop. If the incident did happen, it was to have a profound influence on the success of the voyage, and on the whole future of Captain Kidd. By way of revenge the captain of the sloop seized half the crew and pressed them into government service – leaving Kidd no choice but to pick up a new crew when he reached New York. The replacements were not 'honest tars' – they were hardened criminals and pirates.

In September 1696 Kidd left New York and headed for the Cape of Good Hope, but the voyage was dogged with problems. An attack – possibly of cholera – killed a third of the entire crew when they reached the Comoros Islands off the eastern coast of Africa. To compound matters, Kidd was unable to locate any of the pirates he had been commissioned to hunt down – it turned out that Thomas Tew, his main target, had already been killed. Kidd's men were getting angry at the prospect of not getting any reward or capturing any treasure, and matters came to a head when they encountered a Dutch merchant ship.

The crew wanted to attack her, whereas Kidd knew that this would be an act of piracy – and one not likely to be popular with the Dutch-born King William III, who had signed the Letter of Marque. An argument broke out during which Kidd threw an iron bucket at a gunner called William Moore. The gunner fell to the deck with a fractured skull, and died a few days later. Technically this was murder, but Kidd was confident that he could explain away his actions at a later date.

At the end of January 1698 Kidd's fortunes appeared to have changed. He caught up with an Armenian ship operating off the coast of India – the 400-ton *Quedagh Merchant*, loaded with extremely valuable silks, satins, muslins, as well as gold, silver, and an incredible assortment of East Indian merchandise. A later deposition to the court in London refers to '1200 Bayles of Muslins raw silk and Callicoes of all sorts fourteen hundred baggs of brown Sugars 84 Bayles of raw silke and eighty Chests of Opium besides iron and other goods', including diamonds, rubies, gold bars, and so on.

The captain of *Quedagh Merchant* was an Englishman named Wright, who had purchased passes from the French East India Company promising him the protection of the French Crown. Kidd wanted to return the ship to the captain because he was English, but the crew were having none of it. They argued that because the *Quedagh Merchant* was carrying French passes she was therefore as good as being French – and was thus a fair target.

In an attempt to maintain control over his crew, Kidd relented and kept the prize. When this news reached England, it confirmed Kidd's reputation as a pirate, and various naval commanders were ordered to 'pursue and seize the said Kidd and his accomplices' for the 'notorious piracies' which they had committed. Kidd kept the French passes of the *Quedagh Merchant*, as well as the vessel itself – which he renamed the *Adventure Prize*, and off he sailed to Madagascar to hunt down more pirates. He also succeeded in selling some of the cargo – particularly the fabrics and the sugar, raising some £7,000.

By coincidence the only pirate he came across on Madagascar was Captain Robert Culliford – the man who had stolen Kidd's ship back in Antigua. But when Kidd ordered his crew to attack Culliford's ship his crew refused – and indeed all but thirteen crew members deserted Kidd and joined Culliford, taking with them their share of the proceeds of the captured cargo. Grossly under-manned, Kidd sailed the *Adventure Prize* back to the Caribbean only to discover that he was a wanted criminal. He was lured back to New York by the governor, the Earl of Bellomont, who promised Kidd clemency.

However, the Earl must have been concerned to distance himself from Kidd – he was after all an investor in the project, and must have been worried that he would be implicated in the charge of piracy. He therefore had Kidd arrested and thrown in prison, along with his wife Sarah, and they languished there for over a year until Kidd was put on board a ship bound for London, where he was to be hauled before Parliament to answer questions about his conduct.

Afterwards he was carted off to the Admiralty Court to face trial, where he learned for the first time that he was to be charged with murder.

Political shenanigans now came to the surface. There was no way that Kidd was going to get a fair trial. The two French passes, which at least went some way to justifying Kidd's actions in seizing the *Quedagh Merchant*, mysteriously went missing from the trial papers and were not found for another two centuries, among Admiralty documents.

Various crew members were given pardons in exchange for telling the court about Kidd's barbarity and cruelty – and of course his murder of William Moore. In the event he was found guilty on one charge of murder and five charges of piracy – and in 1701 was sentenced to death by hanging.

Six of his fellow pirates were also sentenced to be executed, but unlike Kidd all of them were pardoned at the last moment. During the hanging, at London's Execution Docks in Wapping, the hangman's rope broke. Even this did not spare Kidd, and he was hanged at the second attempt. His body was gibbeted – in other words left hanging, bound in chains, on the banks of the Thames for almost three years as a warning to other sailors.

What then of his buried treasure? It is known that Kidd had buried a small part of the treasure on Gardiners Island near New York – but that was dug up and used as evidence against him in his trial. No further treasure has been found, and Kidd has to remain one of the unluckiest men ever convicted of piracy – he was left to hang out to dry by a government which wanted to disassociate itself from something which was very much a problem of its own making.

Kidd's fate showed how piracy and politics were irretrievably inter-twined. He was never a particularly successful plunderer of other ships, he showed weakness when faced with a recalcitrant crew, and he lacked judgment. His misdeeds were nothing like as inexcusable and illegal as those of many other pirates, but the government needed a scapegoat and Kidd was in the wrong place at the wrong time.

*****

Henry Avery (otherwise Every)

Next up, from the end of the middle phase of the Golden Age, a man who was altogether more successful – in fact someone who has a claim to 'the most successful pirate ever' – and one who disappeared without trace. His name was Henry Avery, sometimes spelled Every, and he is believed to have lived between 1659 and 1700.

He used several aliases throughout his career, including Benjamin Bridgeman, and was known as Long Ben to his crewmen and associates.

Little is known about his upbringing and early career. He is believed to have been born in Newton Ferrers, near Plymouth, and joined the Royal Navy. Subsequently he began slave trading along the western coast of Africa.

In 1693, he was employed as first mate aboard the warship *Charles II*, which had been commissioned by the Spanish king – at that stage an ally of Britain – to prey on French vessels in the West Indies. Working for a foreign power was not easy – the sailors demanded that they be paid every six months, rather than at the end of the voyage as was customary, and after six months they had still got no further than the northern Spanish harbour of La Coruña, where other vessels were assembling for the expedition. The crew got fed up with waiting to be paid. Madrid failed to come up either with wages or a Letter of Marque to enable them to start privateering, so in May 1794 the restless sailors mutinied. Having seized the ship they renamed her *Fancy*, and Avery was elected as the new captain. The decision was made to join the 'pirate round'.

They travelled down the west coast of Africa, capturing and pillaging a number of merchant ships off the Cape Verde Islands before rounding the Cape and heading for Madagascar. By then Avery had picked up a number of discontented sailors from other ships and by the time the Fancy reached Madagascar in mid-1695, it was a floating rogues' gallery of some 150 men.

Avery had learned that a Mughal Empire fleet was soon to set sail from the Red Sea port of Mocha, in modern day Yemen, on a voyage home to Surat in India. As well as carrying Muslim pilgrims returning from their hajj to Mecca, the armada would also include several heavily laden merchant vessels and treasure ships owned by the Great Mughal of India himself.

Avery joined forces with the notorious pirate Thomas Tew, in charge of the *Amity*, with sixty pirates on board. Other buccaneers such as Joseph Faro on the *Portsmouth Adventure*, Richard Want on the *Dolphin*, William Mayes on the *Pearl* and Thomas Wake on the *Susanna* also joined the fleet of ambushers. Together they set up patrols across the entrance to the Red Sea, waiting for the Mughal fleet to set sail.

All of these buccaneers had privateering commissions from all across the Eastern seaboard of the North American colonies, and, so as far as they were concerned, they were privateers not pirates. Nevertheless, they elected Avery as their leader.

In August 1695 they saw what they were waiting for – a fleet of twenty-five ships returning to India laden with valuable cargoes. Tew in the *Amity* was the first to catch up with a lumbering escort vessel called the *Fath Mah Ma-madi*. Unfortunately, Tew was killed right at the start of the action and his dispirited crew immediately surrendered and were taken on board the *Fath Mah Ma-madi* as prisoners.

However, a few days later Avery successfully caught up with the *Fath Mah Ma-madi* and after a short battle the ship surrendered and was relieved of some £50,000 worth of gold and silver. Tew's men were released.

Avery and his crew, with their three remaining ships, resumed the hunt for the main treasure fleet. On 7 September they caught up with the richest prize in the Indian fleet: the Great Mughal flagship *Ganj-i-Sawai*. It was the biggest ship in the whole of India, and boasted several dozen cannon and a complement of 400 riflemen – more than the entire pirate fleet combined.

Captain Avery gambled on an attack, and immediately scored a devastating blow when one of his first cannon volleys smashed into the *Ganj-i-Sawai's* mainmast and brought it crashing down. Effectively this meant that the ship could no longer manoeuvre. To make matters worse, the Indian defenders fell into disarray after one of their artillery pieces malfunctioned and exploded.

Avery drew up alongside the stricken ship in the *Fancy* and sent on a boarding party, and after a fierce hand-to-hand fight the Indian soldiers were driven back. Before long the *Ganj-i-Sawai* had been captured.

The pirates sacked the ship and brutalised its passengers. Avery had captured up to £600,000 in precious metals and jewels, making him the richest pirate in the world, equivalent to around £55,000,000 in today's money.

Afterwards, Avery and his crew tortured and killed a great number of the passengers and carried out widespread rapes on women of all ages.

There were accounts of women stabbing themselves with daggers or jumping overboard, preferring to drown rather than to being defiled by heathen pirates.

When news of the attack reached the ears of the Great Mughal in India he was incandescent at the loss – and in particular at the disgraceful torture and rape of members of his own family. He briefly arrested officials from the British East India Company, who had promised to safeguard Indian shipping, and he threatened to destroy the British settlement of Bombay unless the Company paid compensation.

Putting it in context, the entire profits of the East India Company in the previous year had slumped to £30,000. Suddenly they were being asked to stump up compensation of £350,000 – or face losing their trading monopoly. Bluntly, they had no choice but to pay up.

At the same time the East India Company posted a reward – initially £500 but later increased by the Privy Council to £1,000 – for information leading to the arrest of Avery. However, Avery and his crew were nowhere to be seen. According to one report, he persuaded the other pirate ships to leave the captured treasure on board the *Fancy*, ready to be divided up in the morning. One story suggests that he slipped away in the night and set a course for the Caribbean, keeping all the treasure to himself and his crew. Each crew member received over £1,000 (perhaps equivalent to £100,000 today). This was far more money than most sailors ever made in their lifetime and in addition to the pure gold, each received a portion of the huge haul of gemstones which had been captured.

For someone with a price on his head, Avery's feat in navigating undetected halfway across the world was an enormous achievement. The ship called in at Ascension Island – then uninhabited – to try to get fresh water and supplies, and then continued towards the West Indies. The pirates no longer favoured Jamaica, where British rule had been re-imposed. First of all, they called in at St Thomas, in the Virgin Islands, where they were able to sell some of their goods and to re-provision. By March 1696 they had moved on to the almost deserted and pirate-friendly islands of the Bahamas. Here, the supposedly British administration was in total disarray and corruption was rife.

Upon arriving at New Providence in the Bahamas, they posed as slavers and bribed the island's governor, a man by the name of Trott, into letting them come ashore. Avery handed over to Trott the battle-scarred *Fancy* and a small fortune in ivory tusks. From Trott's point of view, the bribe of £850 in cash was three times his annual salary – and giving the pirates shelter actually boosted the island's defensive strength against the French Navy, who were reportedly seeking to capture New Providence.

Trott later claimed he had no idea that Avery was a pirate – by then Avery was using the name Bridgeman – but the presence of a large number of Indian coins being used in the local bars and brothels must have given some clue as to where the money came from. The offer of a reward had led to the first worldwide manhunt in recorded history, but astonishingly Avery managed to disappear into thin air. He was helped in this by Trott, who gave Avery warning that the authorities were closing in on him. To cover his tracks Trott even issued warrants for the arrest of Avery and his men – about 100 in all. In order to cover up his own involvement in the bribe, he destroyed the *Fancy*.

Avery's men adopted aliases and went their separate ways – some remaining in the Caribbean and others travelling up to the American colonies, and others returning to Britain where in time, over twenty-four were arrested and six were brought to trial. To the horror of the government of the day all six were acquitted, so they were immediately re-arrested, charged with a different offence of stealing the original ship, and told that the burden of proof was on them to prove their innocence 'because the change of name from the *Charles II* to the *Fancy* spoke for itself'.

In other words, the Law was determined to get revenge. All six were convicted, and hanged in London in November 1696. The reports of the trial became bestsellers, and of course speculation immediately started: where had all the money gone? And also, what of Avery? He was never caught and vanished from all records after 1696.

His fate remains a complete mystery. One report was that he sailed to Ireland under the name 'Bridgeman', but his trail goes cold from there.

Most of his contemporaries believed he made a clean getaway and retired with his loot. A few fictional works even described him as starting his own pirate utopia on Madagascar, giving rise to the woodcut at the end of the chapter showing Avery, striding round in the dress of an English gentleman, with a slave holding a sunshade over his head.

There were even rumours that he styled himself King of Madagascar. Years later, another tale would surface, claiming that Avery had returned to his native England to settle down, only to be bilked out of his fortune by corrupt diamond merchants in Bristol. According to that version, the so-called 'King of the Pirates' died in Barnstaple in North Devon, poor and anonymous, 'not being worth as much as would buy him a coffin'.

Whatever may have happened to him, many believe that his treasure is still out there somewhere and the fact that he was never caught helped fire the public imagination. Somehow, along the way the murders and the rapes got overlooked.

Whereas the British Crown despised Avery, he had become a folk hero among the population – a sort of Robin Hood. Almost single-handedly he revitalised piracy throughout the world as many out-of-work sailors could see the potential riches that could be obtained through piracy.

It is highly probable that hearing the stories of Henry Avery inspired sailors such as Edward 'Blackbeard' Teach and Benjamin Hornigold, who are mentioned later in Part Two. As a testament to his legacy as 'the pirate king' many pirates often named their ships the *Fancy* in homage to his great pirate ship. Avery's fame was cemented in sea shanties such as *The Ballad of Long Ben* and by books such as Daniel Defoe's *The King of Pirates*, as well as in plays such as Johnson's 1712 stage production of *The Successful Pyrate*. All these stories seem to stem from a fictionalised biography by Dutchman Adrian van Broeck (which is believed to have been a pseudonym) entitled *The Life and Adventures of Capt. John Avery; the Famous English Pirate, Now in Possession of Madagascar*, which was published in 1709. Thanks to this book Avery's life became sensationalised and exaggerated, and put forward the idea that Avery ended up as King of Madagascar, minting his own coins, living in a palace, commanding an army of 15,000 pirates and with forty warships at his disposal. It was of course utter hogwash, but the public loved it.

***

What conclusions can be drawn from these three stories? It is perhaps necessary to remove Captain Morgan from the equation because he was so atypical. Yes, he plundered; yes, he was motivated by self-interest; yes, he broke the law. But he also displayed an element of altruism missing from most of his contemporaries – he wanted to make Jamaica safe. In doing so he would not only advance his own interests as a plantation owner, but he would also protect English interests in the entire region. Besides, his activities have more to do with military campaigns than mere acts of piracy – he was not interested in lying in wait for one or two merchant ships, and stealing their cargo. His campaigns were against cities – he extorted ransom, he seized slaves, he stole cattle, he did anything which damaged Spanish interests, especially if in doing so he advanced his own.

Morgan therefore stands apart from his contemporaries, a 'gentleman thief' in the mould of Sir Francis Drake. Above all he was a man who made sure that he had the friendship and support of those in authority, and that when the chips were down this friendship and loyalty meant that he received a telling-off, but never serious punishment. Indeed, when he was brought back to London for trial, he was really only put under house arrest, never incarcerated in the Tower like the unfortunate Modyford. Yet the fact that he was recalled at all shows how buccaneers were always vulnerable to acts of political expediency. They were never really masters of their own destiny. That was certainly true of Kidd – he was sacrificed because the government wanted to make an example out of him – and the Admiralty were perfectly willing to manipulate the evidence, and obtain false testimony, in order to get a result.

Avery was also an oddball in the sense that he knew when to stop, getting out at the top. Most other pirates carried on and on, until they were stopped in their tracks by death (natural or otherwise). For the vast majority of buccaneers in the seventeenth and eighteenth centuries, their careers were remarkably short, usually ending on the gallows, or by illnesses such as typhus, yellow fever and scurvy (all of them spreading like wildfire in the cramped conditions on board). If they survived disease, they still had to contend with storms and natural disasters. They needed the good fortune to escape the predations of other pirates intent on claiming a bounty by seizing them and their ships – and they had to be lucky in battle, unlike Thomas Tew, killed by a cannon shot in the opening salvo of an attack.

An illustration showing Avery enjoying a regal existence on Madagascar, dressed as an English gentleman and being protected from the sun by a slave holding aloft a parasol.

Part Two

THE BEGINNING OF THE END OF THE GOLDEN AGE

Chapter 4

Parliament, Proclamations and Pardons

A number of things had to fall in place before the scourge of piracy could be eradicated – the most important being a real determination on the part of the authorities. For some years they had tried to get round a major difficulty: in almost every case the act of piracy took place half a world away – in the Caribbean, or off Madagascar, or off the coast of South America. Yet the legislation dealing with piracy was enacted in the reign of Henry VIII and reflected the fact that at that stage there were no colonies – and therefore no colonial administration or system of justice. In 1698 the government decided to modify the legislation to allow piracy trials to take place where the crime had actually been committed. The Piracy Act, or to give it its full title 'An Act for the more effectual suppression of Piracy', came into force in 1700. The legislation is interesting because it sets out the nature of the problem, as seen by the legislators.

The Act starts with a recital of the dangers and difficulties:

Whereas by the Offences at Sea Act 1536, it is enacted, that treasons, felonies, robberies, murders, and confederacies committed on the sea, shall be enquired of, tried, and determined according to the common course of the laws of this land used for such offences upon the land within this realm; whereupon the trial of those offenders before the admiral, or his lieutenant, or his commissary, hath been altogether disused...

In other words, prosecutions for piracy had ceased because of the cost of bringing the accused, and witnesses, back to England. The Act continues:

And whereas, that since the making of the said Act, and especially of late years, it hath been found by experience, that persons committing piracies, robberies, and felonies on the seas, in or near the East and West Indies, and in places very remote, cannot be brought to condign [appropriate] punishment without great trouble and charges in sending them into England to be tried within the realm, as the said statute directs, insomuch that many idle and profligate persons have been thereby encouraged to turn pirates, and betake themselves to that sort of wicked life, trusting that they shall not, or at least cannot easily, be questioned for such their piracies and robberies, by reason of the great trouble and expence that will necessarily fall upon such as shall attempt to apprehend and prosecute them for the same.

This shows that Parliament recognised that pirates were happily flouting the law because they knew that they were in effect immune from prosecution by reason of the cost and delays in bringing charges against them.

And whereas the numbers of them are of late very much increased, and their insolencies so great, that unless some speedy remedy be provided to suppress them, by a strict and more easy way for putting the ancient laws in that behalf in execution, the trade and navigation into remote parts will very much suffer thereby; Be it therefore declared and enacted...

This was therefore official recognition that things had got a lot worse and that Britain's trade interests were being put at serious risk.

The actual change in the law enacted was that henceforth all acts of piracy could be:

examined, inquired of, tried, heard and determined, and adjudged in any place at sea, or upon the land, in any of his Majesty's islands, plantations, colonies, dominions, forts, or factories.

This enabled admirals to hold a court session to hear the trials of pirates in any place they deemed necessary, rather than requiring that the trial be held in England. It got round the problem of having to locate victims and bring them back to attend a trial in London; it simplified getting hold of witnesses. Above all, it made the punishment and the crime much more closely connected – and for that reason the punishment was all the more effective. It established the death penalty for piracy – and the very public hangings which resulted certainly acted as a deterrent.

The Admiralty Courts set up pursuant to the new Act may have taken a while to get going, but in due course transformed the anti-piracy movement. It has been estimated that over 400 pirates were sent to the gallows as a result of courts held in places as far apart as West Africa, the American colonies and the Caribbean. In the aftermath of the naval mission led by Captain Ogle in the *Swallow* which resulted in the death of the notorious Bartholomew Roberts in 1722 the Admiralty Court which was held at Cape Corso in West Africa dealt with hundreds of men taken prisoner and brought for trial. Just seventy-four were acquitted, while fifty-two were convicted and hanged outside the castle gates. Many of them were in their twenties, several as young as 21, the oldest 45. In two cases sentence was 'respited till the King's pleasure is further known', and another twenty were sentenced to seven years servitude – hard labour in the mines on the Cape Coast operated by the Royal Africa Company. Another seventeen were sent back to London to be kept in Marshalsea Prison awaiting further trial. Thirty-two died before they were tried, and the seventy negroes captured by Ogle were released without charge.

It marked a significant turning point – the navy had shown that it alone could take on the pirate ships and win, and the courts showed that they had the determination to punish swiftly and severely. Ogle went on to be knighted, becoming known as Sir Chaloner Ogle, and was the only person to receive the honour specifically as a result of anti-piracy activities.

The 1698 Act of Parliament specified that the commissions of enquiry investigating an act of piracy were to consist of a minimum of seven men – and specified that only:

known merchants, factors, or planters, or such as are captains, lieutenants, or warrant officers in any of his majesty's ships of war, or captains, masters, or mates of some English ship, shall be capable of being so called, and sitting and voting in the said court.

Strict rules on evidence, procedure and on swearing the oath were also laid down. The statute also granted the commissioners of these vice-admiralty courts 'full power and authority' to issue warrants, summon the necessary witnesses, and 'to do all things necessary for the hearing and final determination of any case of piracy, robbery, or felony.'

The Act made it clear that there had been a problem with people aiding and abetting pirates. As the Act puts it:

several evil-disposed persons, in the plantations and elsewhere, have contributed very much towards the increase and encouragement of pirates, by setting them forth, and by aiding abetting, receiving, and concealing them and their goods.

The Act promptly made this an offence punishable by death and went on to create the offence of being an accessory – something which also carried the death penalty. The wording expressly stated:

And further, that after any piracy or robbery is or shall be committed by any pirate or robber whatsoever, every person and persons, who knowing that such pirate or robber has done or committed such piracy and robbery, shall on the land or upon the sea, receive, entertain or conceal any such pirate or robber, or receive or take into his custody any ship, vessel, goods or chattels, which have been by any such pirate or robber piratically and feloniously taken, shall be and are hereby likewise declared, deemed and adjudged to be accessary to such piracy and robbery.

What this meant was that there was no distinction between the person committing the piracy, or one offering him refuge, or hiding his goods. Anyone associated with piracy was liable to be hanged, and the death penalty remained in operation until it was abolished by the Piracy Act of 1837.

Recognising that pursuing pirates was a dangerous business, the Act also established that rewards were to be granted to:

Commanders, Masters, and other Officers, Seamen, and Mariners, as shall either bravely defend their own Ships, or take, seize and destroy pirates.

The legislators clearly felt that the pirate body was made up of people who were originally merchant seamen, and the legislation expressly took away all rights to be paid a wage for the time when a deserter had been in legitimate service. As it says:

for the prevention of seamen deserting of merchant ships abroad in parts beyond the seas, which is the chief occasion of their turning pirates, and of great detriment to trade and navigation in general; Be it enacted by the authority aforesaid, that all such seamen, officers or sailors, who shall desert the ships or vessels wherein they are hired to serve for that voyage, shall for such offence forfeit all such wages as shall be then due to him or them.

The Act is interesting because in addressing certain concerns it shows that these matters were prevalent and were deemed important enough to legislate against. So, plantation owners who failed to cooperate with the terms of the Act were liable to have their plantations confiscated. Captains of ships who marooned their sailors and failed to bring them home were liable to three months imprisonment.

In practice, the Act had little or no immediate effect. Britain's navy had its hands full fighting 'Queen Anne's War' – as the War of Spanish Succession was known in its North American context. It was not until after the Treaty of Utrecht in 1713 that Her Majesty's Navy was able to turn its attention to the growing menace posed, especially in the Caribbean and in the lawless islands of the Bahamas where the so-called 'Commonwealth of Pirates' operated. In the Bahamas there were no government ships, and the pirates far outnumbered the island's population of legitimate settlers. The interruptions to free trade grew ever more frequent, and when the new Hanoverian King George succeeded to Queen Anne's throne he was persuaded to issue a Proclamation a year after his accession. It is worth stating in full, because like the earlier statute, it sets out the concerns as well as establishing a Royal Pardon, along with further rewards for the capture of pirates and their ships. The Proclamation, which appeared in the London Gazette, was prefaced with a statement as follows:

Complaint having been made to His Majesty, by great Numbers of Merchants, Masters of Ships, and others, as well as by the several Governours of His Majesty's Islands and Plantations in the West-Indies, that the Pirates are grown so numerous that they infest not only the Seas near Jamaica, but even those of the Northern Continent of America; and that unless some effectual Means be used, the whole Trade from Great Britain to those Parts will not only be obstructed, but in imminent danger of being lost: His Majesty has, upon mature Deliberation in Council, been graciously pleased, in the first Place, to order a proper force to be employed for suppressing the said Piracies; which Force so to be employed as follows... :

By the King, A PROCLAMATION for the Suppressing of Pyrates:

Whereas we have received information, that several Persons, Subjects of Great Britain, have, since the 24th Day of June, in the Year of our Lord, 1715, committed divers Pyracies and Robberies upon the High-Seas, in the West Indies, or adjoyning to our Plantations, which hath and may Occassion great Damage to the Merchants of Great Britain, and others trading unto those Parts; and tho' we have appointed such a Force as we judge sufficient for suppressing the said Pyrates, yet the more effectually to put an End to the same, we have thought fit, by and with the Advice of our Privy Council, to Issue this our Royal Proclamation; the said Pyrates, shall on, or before, the 5th of September, in the year of our Lord 1718, surrender him or themselves, to one of our Principal Secretaries of State in Great Britain or Ireland, or to any Governor or Deputy Governor of any of our Plantations beyond the Seas; every such Pyratee and Pyrates so surrendering him, or themselves, as aforesaid, shall have our gracious Pardon, of, and for such, his or their Pyracy, or Piracies, by him or them committed, before the fifth of January next ensuing. And we do hereby strictly charge and command all our Admirals, Captains, and other Officers at Sea, and all our Governors and Commanders of any Forts, Castles, or other Places in our Plantations, and all other our Officers Civil and Military, to seize and take such of the Pyrates, who shall refuse or neglect to surrender themselves accordingly.

What this meant is that for the first time an amnesty was on offer, provided it was taken up within fifteen months. It also imposed a duty on naval commanders and colonial leaders alike to seize pirates operating in their area. The Proclamation continued:

And we do hereby further declare, that in Case any Person or Persons, on, or after, the 6th day of September, 1718, shall discover or seize, or cause or procure to be discovered or seized, any one or more of the said Pyrates, so refusing or neglecting to surrender themselves as aforesaid, so as they may be brought to Justice, and convicted of the said Offence, such Person or Persons, so making such Discovery or Seizure, or causing or procuring such Discovery or Seizure to be made, shall have and receive as a Reward for the same, viz. for every Commander of any private Ship or Vessel, the Sum of £100; for every Lieutenant, Master, Boatswain, Carpenter and Gunner, the sum of £40; for every inferior officer, the Sum of £30 and for every private Man the Sum of £20. And if any Person or persons, belong to, and being Part of the Crew, of any Pyrate Ship or Vessel, so as he or they be brought to Justice, and be convicted of the said Offence, such Person or Persons, as a Reward for the same, shall receive for every such Commander, the Sum of £200 which said Sums, the Lord Treasurer, or the Commissioners of our Treasury for the time being, are hereby required, and desired to pay accordingly.

A reward of £200 was quite an incentive for pirates to 'shop' their fellow-pirates and would certainly have made many captains nervous about the continuing reliability of their crews. Equally, the payment of a reward of £100 was a powerful incentive for bounty hunters who wanted to try their luck. Linked to the Proclamation, the government specified a number of ships to be sent to police the main trouble spots. Most important of all, the king promised to send a force to destroy the very heart of the pirate empire – their lawless base on New Providence Island in the Bahamas.

The Proclamation was issued from Hampton Court on 5 September 1717, but there were no naval ships crossing the Atlantic at that time and it was not until the first week in December 1717 that news finally reached Boston. The Proclamation was then printed in the 9 December edition of the *Boston News Letter*. From Boston the news was slowly disseminated throughout the colonies and islands in the Caribbean. From Bermuda, printed transcripts of the Proclamation were delivered by sloop to the Bahamas, where the news was received with mixed results. For some it was the news they had been waiting for – a chance to 'come home' – the slate wiped clean. For others, especially Charles Vane, it was seen as a derisory offer, a sign that the government knew their position was weak and had to resort to bribery. If anything, it emboldened men like Vane, Blackbeard and Bonnet. Sure, they were happy to pay lip-service to the idea of a pardon, but in reality they were not about to just give up their profitable lifestyle. What happened next is largely tied up in the remarkable story of Woodes Rogers, set out in the Chapter 7. He arrived on New Providence Island on 26 July 1718, and it was to prove the beginning of the end for the 'Commonwealth of Pirates' and their Golden Age.

Meanwhile back in London the news of the Proclamation was made known to merchants via the London Gazette. In its edition of 28 June 1718 it informed readers that Captain Pearse had arrived at New Providence Island on board the *Phoenix* four months earlier and that since that date,

> *Captains Hornigold, Nichols, Burgess, Lesley, and 114 of their Company had surrendered themselves …and accepted His Majesty's Proclamation for Suppressing the Pirates; that others came in daily; and that he hoped in a little time to disperse all the Pirates on that island.*

A reminder that the loss of a limb was not uncommon – here, a one-legged sailor acts as cook.

Chapter 5

Rotten to the Core, Colonial Governors and Plantation Owners

Dr Samuel Johnson wrote a political tract, published in Dublin in 1777, in which he discussed the role of colonial settlements. He wrote:

> *That such a settlement may be of use in war, no man …. will deny. But war is not the whole business of life, it happens but seldom, and every man either good or wise wishes its frequency still less…. The advantage of a settlement in time of peace is I think not easily so proved. For what use can it have but as a station for contraband traders, a nursery of fraud and a receptacle of theft?*

He went on to consider the role of the British government in looking after such settlements:

> *to pardon a pirate may be injurious to mankind; but how much greater is the crime of opening a port in which all pirates shall be safe? The contraband trader is not more worthy of protection; if he … trades by force he is a pirate; if he trades secretly he is only a thief. Those who honestly refuse his traffick he hates as obstructors of his profit; and those with whom he deals he cheats, because he knows that they dare not complain.*

As it happens Dr Johnson was writing about the Falkland Islands, but the concerns applied equally to any trading station in the world. Left un-policed, they were bound to become havens for the lawless. The honest trader would lose out because he would not be able to compete with smuggled or stolen goods being sold on the black-market.

The link between piracy and smuggling existed on different levels – pirates were not averse to hijacking smuggled goods, and smugglers and corrupt officials were needed to help unload stolen cargoes, at the same time as evading paying customs duties. The connection between piracy, dishonest merchants and tax evasion was clear – and it was helped in the early years of colonial expansion by a frankly disastrous series of appointments at key levels of the administration, starting with the governor. The island governors were, by and large, chosen from the more influential families on those islands. In other words, they had a vested interest in profits from trade. Their loyalty was often to their particular island or region, rather than to the more nebulous concept of 'the Empire'.

The pirates were not of course concerned with the morality of taxation, used to fund the colonial administration. They had no altruistic or political motives – they simply wanted to make lots of money from stealing. But they were undoubtedly helped, especially in the seventeenth century, by the opposition of colonists towards what were known as the Navigation Acts. These statutes, dating back to 1651 during the time of Cromwell's Commonwealth and continuing into the reign of Charles II, were significant in that they were brought in to enhance England's imperial interests. They were there to make profits for the Mother Country, not for the benefit of the colonists. The underlying philosophy was expressed by Lord Chatham, who famously remarked that 'the only use of the American colonies is the monopoly of their consumption and the carriage of their produce'.

The Navigation Acts, embracing a concept termed 'mercantalism', were a collection of laws designed to achieve three things. First, they stated that all goods travelling to and from the colonies had to be carried on English ships – or on colonial ones where three-quarters of the crew were English. Second, the Acts established a list of items known as 'enumerated goods', which could not be sold on to other countries outside the empire without first being passed into an English port where the appropriate duty could be collected. Finally, the Staples Act, passed in 1663, insisted that the majority of goods imported from Europe into the colonies had to come from England.

Not surprisingly, the colonists hated these rules and with the active connivance of the colonial governors, customs officers and so on, did their best to get around the controls. The Dutch, in particular, were active in smuggling manufactured goods into the Caribbean islands, to the extent that by the reign of William III (1688–1702) officials were reporting that European goods could be bought thirty to forty per cent more cheaply from the Dutch than from the English. Tea was smuggled almost as much as any other commodity, and considerable quantities of molasses intended for England managed to find trade outlets in contravention of the Acts.

Doing so meant there were officials and governors willing either to overlook or in some cases actively to participate in the illegal act, be it smuggling or piracy. William Berkeley of Virginia, otherwise a God-fearing and thoughtful individual, was happy to turn a blind eye as long as the interests of the fledgling tobacco interests of Virginia were enhanced. Christopher Codrington, based initially in Barbados and then on Antigua, in the Leeward Islands, introduced sugar production rather than tobacco cultivation to the island and in doing so actively encouraged illicit trade. Rather more corrupt, Benjamin Fletcher the Governor of New York between 1692 and 1697, looked to piracy as the main tool to wrest supremacy from Boston and Philadelphia and to make New York the main seaport on the eastern coast of America.

Pirates flooded in, bringing desperately needed wealth to the colony. Anglo–French hostilities meant that Letters of Marque were being issued like confetti, and the privateers were none too particular whether they captured ships flying one country's flag or another; what they wanted was to cut out the duty under the Letter of Marque about returning captured goods for adjudication by the Admiralty Court, and instead to sell the cargo in some friendly base. None proved more friendly than New York under Fletcher. Bribes were widespread, and the city's financiers grew rich on sponsoring pirate voyages. Fletcher personally encouraged pirates such as Thomas Tew and William Kidd, and was happy to sell Letters of Marque to anyone willing to pay. He is alleged to have been associated with at least sixteen voyages to Madagascar to trade with pirates based there (known colloquially as 'the Red Sea trade') – all of them involving Fletcher being paid a share of the illegal profits. Fletcher was also accused of interference in elections as well as arbitrary treatment of opponents, of mishandling military funds and accepting bribes. He was accused of excessive land grants and of giving protection to pirates. His recall to London was demanded 'gently or in disgrace, if we be rid of him'. Small wonder that he was eventually removed from office, and was replaced as Governor by Richard Coote, Earl of Bellomont.

Interestingly all three governors, Berkeley, Codrington and Fletcher, were devout in their Christian beliefs, but never allowed such beliefs to get in the way of promoting wealth and prosperity, whether by fair means or foul. Fletcher's departure was followed by the sacking of William Markham of Pennsylvania, and the king issued a circular letter to all other colonial governors warning them that if they failed to cooperate and obey the law, they would suffer the same fate.

Another governor to get the sack was Nicholas Trott in the Bahamas. Here, on New Providence Island, before the arrival of Woodes Rogers, Governor Trott had established his own corrupt fiefdom. Receiving a bribe from a man like Henry Avery, mentioned earlier, became part of a pattern of turning a blind eye in return for secret remuneration. So neglectful of his duties had Trott become that by 1713 there were around 1,000 pirates operating from New Providence Island, far outnumbering the original law-abiding population. Not without reason was the island described as 'a sink or nest of infamous rascals'.

By the end of the seventeenth century the British government finally realised that something needed to be done to end the corruption. It was undermining the whole idea of mercantalism and making the authorities look extremely foolish. In the late 1690s, Edward Randolph had been appointed to the post of Surveyor-General of Customs in the American Colonies and was requested by the Lords of Trade and Plantations to carry out a detailed investigation. After inspecting the problem, he came up with a list of problems concerning local merchants in a letter entitled *A Discours About Pyrates, With Proper Remedies To Suppress Them'*.

He wrote:

The chief places where Pyrates Resort & are Harboured, are, as follows: ... Pennsilvania [sic]: Severall of those pyrates ... were, upon an acknowledgement of the Govrs. Favour, permitted to settle & Trade there. Rhode Island Has bin many Years, and still is the Chiefe Refuge for Pyrates. Boston.... Some of the Govrs, have Enrichd themselves by the pyrates.

On another occasion a surveyor in Philadelphia complained:

They walk the streets with their pockets full of gold and are the constant companion of the chief in the government. They threaten my life and those who were active in apprehending them; carry their prohibited goods publicly in boats from one place to another for a market; threaten the lives of the King's Collectors and with force and arms rescue the goods from them. All these parts swarm with pirates, so that if some speedy and effectual course be not taken the trade of America will be ruined.

Randolph offered a number of constructive suggestions. He recommended that:

no person be made Governor in any of the Proprieties, until he be first Approved of by his Majesties Order in Council, as by the Act for Preventing Frauds, and Regulating abuses in the Plantation Trade ... is Enacted.

This latter piece of legislation had been passed in 1696. Randolph also noted a change in the nature of the pirate trade:

In the 1670s I observed that they fitted out vessels of sixty or seventy tons and sent them without commission to the Spanish West Indies, whence they brought home great quantities of silver coins and bullion ... insomuch that the Spanish ambassador complained thereof. But now these pirates have found a more profitable and less hazardous voyage to the Red Sea, where they take from the Moors all they have without resistance and bring it to some one of the plantations in the continent of America or islands adjacent, where they are received and harboured and from whence also they fit out their vessels.

Finally, new and resolutely honest governors transformed the scene and helped greatly to bring about the end of the golden age of piracy, with particular credit going to Alexander Spotswood and Woodes Rogers.

Chapter 6

Governor Alexander Spotswood of Virginia

Alexander Spotswood was born in 1676 in Tangier and was the son of a Scottish army physician. He was an army man through and through. Injured at the Battle of Blenheim, he was at one stage captured and made a prisoner of war. By the time that the War of Spanish Succession ended he had risen to the rank of lieutenant colonel, and on 23 June 1710 took up an appointment as lieutenant governor of Virginia. His twelve-year tenure saw huge changes in the colony, but the changes divided the colonists, some of whom applauded his attempts to limit land grants (especially by exempting speculators and only granting land rights to genuine settlers) while others were appalled at his efforts to control tobacco production and to limit the importance and power of the provincial church. He overhauled the local militia and the system of justice, and in 1716 personally led an expedition which opened up the interior of Virginia by exploring a route through the Blue Ridge Mountains leading into the Shenandoah Valley. But he also riled many other prominent colonists with his tactless and confrontational views. He was, however, resolute in his stand against piracy and smuggling and wrote a whole raft of letters back to the Board of Admiralty, setting out his concerns about the lack of adequate defences. Many of the letters are available online via the Library of Congress, and they give a brilliant insight into how the threats from piracy and smuggling were viewed at the time.

Within two months of his arrival to take up office he was writing to the Commissioners for Trade about local attempts to get round the Navigation Acts:

I have taken care for detecting the persons concerned in carrying on an illegal trade to Curracoa and St. Thomas's, and shall by the next Opportunity give Yo'r Lord'ps a more particular account of my Discoverys in that Affair. It is very apparent that the want of Guard ships here so frequently, has given great encouragement to the carrying on this Trade, and I am informed it has been the practice for Vessells bound to the West Indies (when they found no man of war in the bay) to take in great quantitys of tobacco after they had cleared with the Officer.

Spotswood proposed various administrative changes, but pleaded for more naval protection:

> *in my Opinion nothing can more effectually break that trade than the having Guard ships constantly attending here, and more especially if (according to what I perceive has been often represented by the President and Council) a sloop or other small Vessell well fitted and mann'd were sent hither to attend the Guard-ship; such a vessell would not only be of the greatest use for suppressing the Enemy's Privateers, but would contribute very much to the preventing of illegal Trade.*

In the same letter he continued:

> *The Privateers have proved very trouble some to the Coast this Summer; they have taken a great many Vessells, and kept the Inhabitants about the Capes in continual Alarms after the loss of the Garland and in the absence of the Enterprize, which having gone first to New York to refitt, went afterwards to the Bahama Islands, and is but the other day returned hither. It is a mighty inconvenience that upon any accident to the men of war attending here they are obliged to go to New York to refitt, or, if they want bread or other provisions, they must go there for a Supply, and in their absence the Country is exposed to the insults of every little Privateer, and not any place of Defence, nor one piece of Cannon mounted in the Country to oppose them.*

Spotswood advocated building a fort at Point Comfort – 'the very name of it would strike an awe in the Enemy, it would afford a Retreat for Ships when pursued by Privateers in time of War or by Pirates (which must be expected)'.

He maintained a bombardment of letters to the Commissioners for Customs, asking the Admiralty

> *for a Sloop or other Small Vessell of 8 or ten guns, and proportionably mann'd, to pursue the Enemy Privateers among the Flatts, where a man of War can't come at them. If such a Vessell was appointed here, under a diligent Commander, or one that had some suitable encouragement offered him to quicken him in his duty, I am certain she might be very usefull for preventing illegal Trade by speaking with the smallest trading vessels and Examining their Clearings and thereby detecting frauds, and both these Services being so necessary and important I doubt not the Lords of the Admiralty would be prevailed with to order such a Vessell hither.*

The blizzard of letters appears to have worked: the Admiralty sent two patrol ships, the *Enterprize* and the *Triton's Prize*, enabling Spotswood to write just three months later in 1710 with his grateful thanks:

I found the people for want of Guard-ships labouring under frequent Alarms and terrible apprehensions, sadly discouraged by the Insults and Damages of the Enemy's Privateers, and vext to stand often helpless Spectators of their own Losses; but now it is an extraordinary Satisfaction to me and to the whole Colony, to see all those uneasinesses removed by two Ships so proper for this Coast, and under officers who seem well pleased with their Station. And we beg Yo'r Lord'ps to continue after this manner your protection to a country and trade which is of so great consequence to her Majesty and the Kingdoms of Great Britain.

By 1716 Spotswood was again on the scrounge for naval reinforcements, writing:

The whole Trade of this Continent may be endangered if timely measures be not taken to suppress this growing evil. I hope your Lo[rdshi]ps will, therefore, judge it necessary that another Ship of Force be speedily sent hither to Cruise on this Coast for ye protection of our Merchantmen; And … to attack those pyrates in their Quarters before they grow too formidable.

A year later he was warning that:

The number of Pyrates is greatly increased … it is high time some measures were taken to reduce them, either by force or by an offer of pardon.

And a month after that was writing:

[it is] my humble opinion that some additional Strength of Men of War would be absolutely necessary to be sent to these Plantations for the Security of Trade. Experience has shew'd how just my fears were. Our Capes have been for these six Weeks pass'd in a manner blocked up by those Pyrates.

Enemy privateers remained a problem, as did pirates who loitered off the coast waiting to seize lawful exports, but an incident in May 1720 showed how Spotswood's determination was paying off. He wrote to the Admiralty to say '*I forgot in my last to informe y'r Lord'ps*' that a ship belonging to a Capt. Knott, had been boarded and forced '*by one Callifax, a Pirate*', to sail into Virginian waters, where they were captured by the authorities. Spotswood continued:

Six of them appeared the most profligate Wretches I ever heard of, for, as they behaved themselves with the greatest impudence at the Bar, they were no sooner taken from it than they vented their imprecations on their Judges and all concerned in their prosecution, and vow'd if they were again at liberty they would spare none alive that should fall into their hands. I thought it necessary for the greater Terrour to hang up four of them, in Chains. Two others were executed at the same time, and Two who shew'd a just Abhorrence of their past Crimes, I have, by the advice of the Council, pardoned.

Spotswood, scrupulously honest, was concerned to account for all booty recovered from the pirates. They had apparently been successful the previous year in seizing the *Marques de Campo* off the coast of Africa as well as a number of English Merchant ships in the Caribbean. Locating the booty was not easy, for as Spotswood explained:

The eight Pyrates brought in hither had for their share of the booty three Negro men and a boy, a quantity of Gold dust and Moyders [Moidores] which I have now secured in my hands for his Majesty's use, but as they had found means before they were taken to Lodge a good part of their Effects in the hands of some planters here with whom they got acquainted with; and it is but lately that those Effects have been delivered up after a great deal of search and trouble.

In 1721 Spotswood arranged to have fifty-four guns mounted at the mouths of the rivers York, James and Rappahannock in order to protect the ships which anchored there, thus protecting them from the predations of pirates. By developing these coastal defences Spotswood helped develop the idea that Virginia was an unsafe place for pirates to operate.

In addition to his duties as governor, Spotswood also developed the first major iron foundry operating in Virginia, turning out much-needed metal goods such as pots and kettles, fire-backs and fire dogs. In 1722 he also completed the construction of a suitably imposing residence for the governor, only to find that his power-base had been undermined by James Blair, a prominent member of the Virginia Council. Blair arranged for Spotswood to be replaced as governor and, rather than risk the wrath of the pirates who had sworn to 'get him for what he did to Blackbeard', Spotswood was forced to travel to New York in order to gain safe passage back to England in a naval vessel. Subsequently, he married and returned to Virginia (Spotsylvania County being named after him) and for the rest of his life he remained in the colony as a prominent landowner (80,000 acres) and as an important industrialist (three iron foundries at Tubal). For a period of nine years from 1730 he served as deputy Postmaster General of the Colonies.

While these achievements are impressive, especially set against the corruption and ineffectiveness of some of his predecessors, Spotswood is perhaps best remembered for his determination to bring an end to the activities of Edward Teach, mentioned later. Teach had made a fool of the authorities when he had blockaded the harbour at Charles Town. Spotswood set out on a personal mission to bring Teach to account and at his own expense hired the *Jane* and the *Ranger*, and a number of Royal Navy men, to find out where the notorious pirate was hiding. On 18 November 1718, Lieutenant Robert Maynard was persuaded to carry out the search, even though this was not part of his naval duties. He sailed to Ocracoke Inlet in North Carolina where, on 22 November 1718, Maynard defeated Teach and took many of the pirates prisoner. Unaware of the death of Teach, on 24 November 1718 Spotswood issued a proclamation at the Assembly in Williamsburg offering a personal reward for anyone who brought Teach and the other pirates to justice. His actions against piracy, amounting almost to a vendetta, was an inspiration to other governors, and soon the sound of gallows being erected, usually on the beach midway between the high and low tide mark, became commonplace and an obvious deterrent.

One such instance occurred at Newport, Rhode Island, when in 1723 36 men were tried for piracy, and of these 28 were found guilty and sentenced to be hanged. John Valentine, the Advocate General had opened the case with his explanation of their crime:

> *The crime of piracy is robbery (for piracy is a sea term for robbery) committed within the jurisdiction of admiralty. And a pirate is described to be one who to enrich himself either by surprise or open force, sets upon merchants and others trading by sea, to spoil them of their goods and treasure, often times by sinking their vessels, as the case will come out before you. This sort of criminals are engaged in a perpetual war with every individual, with every state, christian or infidel; they have no country, but by the nature of their guilt, separate themselves, renouncing the benefit of all lawful society, to commit these heinous crimes.*

The first charge was that on 8 May 1723, they:

> *piratically and feloniously did surprise, seize, and take the ship Amsterdam, whereof John Welland was then commander or master, of the burthen of one hundred tons, belonging to his Majesty's good subjects.*

They were accused of taking from the ship three barrels of beef, quantities of gold and silver, and a male slave. Subsequently they sank the ship and for good measure cut off Welland's right ear. The trial also heard that on 10 June of the same year they attacked his Majesty's *Grey-Hound*, commanded by Peter Solgard, wounding seven of his men before being captured. In the event, the trial acquitted eight men on the basis that they had shown that they had been forcibly conscripted into piracy. The other twenty-eight found were found guilty. Two were spared the gallows and in the words of the trial report the rest were 'executed on Friday, July 19th, [1723], at Newport on Rhode Island, at a place called Bulls' (Gravelly) Point, within the flux and reflux of the sea'. Suddenly, Rhode Island's association with piracy was beginning to look less and less attractive....

Chapter 7

A New Breed of Governor, Woodes Rogers

In every good cowboy film there must be a number of bad guys in black hats – the desperadoes intent on destruction and mayhem – and there must be at least one good guy wearing a white hat. He is the hero who lays down his life in pursuit of some noble dream or fine idea, or to save a damsel in distress. In the pirate story, Woodes Rogers was the guy in the white hat, and the pirate hordes, holed up in their stronghold of the damned, were very definitely the bad guys wearing

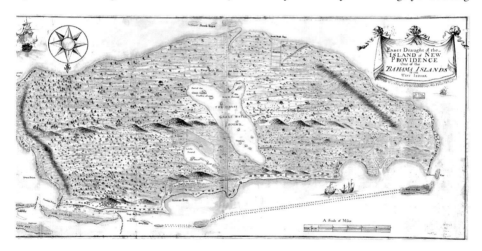

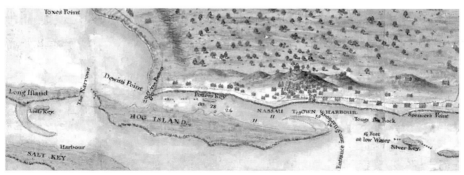

Map of the New Providence Island in the Bahamas.

black. Of course, as it was not Hollywood it was not as clear-cut as that, but the fact remains that Woodes Rogers devoted the best years of his life to eradicating a scourge which he saw as undermining the whole basis on which Britain had become great, that is to say, trade. He got precious little thanks for his efforts, spending time as a bankrupt in prison, but had the satisfaction of knowing that he left the world, and in particular the Caribbean, a better place than when he found it. In 1718 it is estimated that there were at most 2,000 pirates in the Caribbean area. This increased to perhaps 2,500 by 1722 but as piracy started to come under control, and as the pirates dispersed in the face of prolonged naval attrition, numbers dropped to perhaps 500 by 1724. By 1726 there were fewer than 200 pirates left.

Woodes Rogers must take much of the credit for implementing the anti-piracy movement in the area. He arrived in the Bahamas as governor with a reputation of being a man who was used to success: he had already circumnavigated the world, becoming only the third Briton to do so. Not only that but he returned with both his ships intact and with many of his original crew. He had achieved wealth following his capture of the Spanish treasure ship *Nuestra Señora de la Encarnación y Desengaño*. He also achieved fame due to his association with the rescue of Alexander Selkirk (the inspiration for Defoe's story of Robinson Crusoe) and the subsequent publication of his story of the circumnavigation as *A Cruising Voyage Round the World*.

He was a sailor's sailor, a man to be respected by the pirates based in the Bahamas. This was no pen-pusher, no stuffed-shirt bureaucrat. Yet, when he first appeared off the harbour of New Providence island there was little sign of respect from the pirate Charles Vane. He had arrived in harbour shortly before Roger's small trans-Atlantic fleet, having captured a French brigantine loaded with brandy, claret, sugar and indigo. He cheekily sent a message to Rogers saying that if Rogers allowed him to loot and keep the cargo from the captured prize, he would then accept the King's Pardon and retire from piracy. Rogers declined to respond, but had to suffer the humiliation of being unable to enter the harbour and stop the looting. The tides and the shallows in harbour favoured Vane and having looted the captured brigantine he set it adrift, in flames, in the direction of the support vessel *Rose*. The captain of the *Rose* was forced to cut his cables and head out to sea to avoid the flames, but not before Vane had raked the rigging with cannon shot. Rogers was not going to have an easy job in bringing law and order to the pirate's den....

Rogers entered the harbour the following day (27 July 1718) and later wrote that Vane 'with about 90 men ... fled away in a sloop wearing the black flag, and fir'd guns of defiance when they perceived their sloop out-sayl'd the two that I sent to chase them.' Apart from that he met no opposition as he moored his three vessels, the *Rose*, the *Delicia* and the *Milford* and disembarked his independent company of infantrymen, numbering 100, along with a hundred and thirty intrepid colonists. These were Protestants drawn from the Rhineland area of south-west Germany.

Rogers had the sense not to try and take on the whole world at the same time: he picked his time, and he picked his enemies off one by one.

First of all he took possession of the island's dilapidated fort and appointed various key officials from the men he had brought with him: a Chief Justice, Judge of the Admiralty, Customs Collector, and so on. To these six newcomers he added another six from the existing inhabitants to constitute a representative council of twelve people. Rogers had plans for a Bahamian Assembly, made up of fifteen representatives from New Providence, two from Eleuthera and one each from Harbour Island and Abaco. In this way he hoped to ensure that the decisions which he made would be supported in all quarters.

Apart from the pirates he was confronted with multiple problems – the threat of invasion, economic stagnation, disease, and under-manning. New settlers had been avoiding the Bahamas because of the lawlessness, and the residents who were there were indolent, elderly or infirm. When the front of the fort collapsed, there were insufficient labourers to rebuild it. And when a mysterious disease struck the island, believed to be linked to the pile of rotting hides on the harbour foreshore, it led to widespread sickness among almost all of the newcomers, civilian and infantrymen alike. Many died.

Problems were compounded when Rogers was alerted to the fact that the newly appointed governor of Cuba had been charged with the task of eradicating every single one of the Bahamian settlements. An invasion was imminent. The French were also rumoured to have cast a proprietorial eye on the Bahamas and as Rogers said in a letter to the Council: 'They'll not scruple it for the want of title.' French determination to seize the islands was strengthened when news filtered through of the way Vane had seized a French brigantine, when the Emissary allegedly 'stamped his foot and said in a passion that the French King, his Master, had [a] right to these islands and that they would settle here very soon.'

These belligerent threats were one of the reasons why the King's Pardon had been proclaimed the previous year – Britain desperately needed experienced sailors to man its ships. The pirates were nothing if not experienced sailors – and of course chasing pirates tied up Royal Navy personnel and equipment playing 'cat and mouse games' when they could be better used safeguarding the colonists by defending them from attack. One of those who accepted the pardon was Benjamin Hornigold, and he was immediately employed by Rogers to go off and hunt down Vane, and any other pirates he came across and to bring them to face justice. Hornigold did not return for some time, and Rogers must have feared that Hornigold had reneged on the terms of his pardon, or alternatively had been captured by Vane. When he did return, Hornigold brought not Vane but Nicholas Woodall, the captain of the sloop *Woolfe* which had been trading with Vane. Woodall was clapped in irons ready to be sent back on the next ship for England to face trial.

Rogers split his militia up into three groups and established a small fort with eight guns at the eastern end of the harbour. He was faced with a third threat – from Vane. As Rogers noted:

> *This Vaine had the impudence to send me word that he designs to burn my guardship and visit me very soon to return the affront I gave him on my arrival in sending two sloops after him instead of answering the letter he sent me.*

When Hornigold returned having captured ten pirates, Rogers felt that his position was strong enough to be able to hold their trial there and then, on the island. He convened the twelve-strong Court of Admiralty, 'by virtue of his commission as Vice Admiral of these Islands'. One man was acquitted but the remaining nine were found guilty and sentenced to die on 12 December 1718. The hangings were to be carried out with a maximum show of strength, with all the militia called out to ensure that no attempt was made to free the convicted criminals. The scaffolding had been erected high up on the ramparts, facing the sea. The prisoners were all to be dispatched together, in a mass hanging which was expected to be watched by hundreds of the islanders, many of them pirates or former pirates.

Some of the accused were penitent and seemed resigned to their fate. Others saw it as an occasion to swagger and display coloured ribbons from their stockings. Some used the opportunity to address their former colleagues, and one of the condemned, Thomas Morris, commented as he climbed the gallows: 'We have a good Governor, but a harsh one.'

It was widely anticipated that Rogers would pardon the pirates at the last moment, but this was not to be. One lad called George Rounsival was pardoned, but the rest were all executed in a very clear display of the Governor's authority and determination.

Tough on one hand, Rogers could also be merciful: he extended the period in which pirates were allowed to surrender. The islanders responded to the threat of imminent invasion from Spain by labouring furiously to rebuild the island fortifications, and before long fifty guns could be brought to bear on any attackers. Upwards of 250 men could be called on to defend the island. In February 1720 a somewhat half-hearted attempt was made by Spanish forces from Cuba to land troops on New Providence, but the threat was repelled. By now Rogers was exhausted, mentally and also financially, for it became clear that he had been financing the defence works out of his own pocket. In the summer of 1721 he returned to England to face his creditors. He was adjudged bankrupt and thrown into prison, a shameful reward for a man who had devoted his energies so selflessly in the interests of the Crown.

Eventually his creditors took pity on Rogers and absolved him from his debts. This was no doubt helped by the fact that once again he was enjoying the status of national hero, by virtue of the praise heaped on him in the recently published *A General History of the Pyrates*. The king awarded him a pension, backdated to 1721, and George II went further and appointed him as governor for a second term. In 1728 Rogers returned to the islands and quickly realised that the defences again needed rebuilding. However, his proposal to levy a local tax to pay for the work was vetoed by the Assembly, and Rogers responded by suspending the Assembly. This precipitated a constitutional crisis which left Rogers worn out and dispirited. His zeal for change and improvement had gone, and before long he headed for Charles Town to recover his health. In the event he returned to Nassau and died on 15 July 1732. By then the world had moved on; the face of New Providence had changed, with new settlers and new industries. War with Spain had ended, the threat of invasion had disappeared – and the pirates had largely faded away, been pardoned, or had died or gone elsewhere. Small wonder that for the next 240 years the official motto of the Bahamas was 'Piracy Expelled, Commerce Restored'.

Paper cut-out showing cannon and militia on shore, and a ship tied up while sailors climb the rigging....

Chapter 8

Sea Changes

Pirate ships, in general, were chosen with one thing in mind – speed. Our image may be of vessels primed for battle, and of pirates spending their time wielding cutlasses in bitter hand-to-hand fighting – but the reality was that for most pirates the object was to avoid having to fight. They sought to capture their enemies through fear and through vastly superior numbers. The typical merchant ship they were attacking might have no more than a dozen crew on board – the pirate ship of comparable size might have four, five, six times that number. They also often worked in groups, emerging from behind small islands or hidden coves in order to pounce on their unsuspecting prey. Governor Hunter wrote from New York in 1712 complaining that: 'This coast has been very much annoyed by a number of small privateers, who by the advantage of their oars and shoal water keep out of the reach of H.M. ships of war.'

The one thing that pirates sought to avoid was open confrontation with the heavily armed (but perhaps slower) ships of the Navy. In general, the pirates used three different classes of ship – the sloop, the schooner and the brigantine. The sloop would be anything from 30 to 50 ft in length and was the workhorse of pirate fleets. It accounted for almost half of all pirate attacks on shipping in the Caribbean and off the east coast of America during the reign of George I. The early favourite was the Jamaican sloop, made of red cedar, but later operators preferred the Bermuda or jib-headed sloop, because of its speed and handling. Fast (with a top speed of over ten knots) and highly manoeuvrable, she would typically need a crew of a minimum of twenty men. However, on a pirate ship, seventy men were not unusual. She drew 8ft, a depth which enabled her to navigate the shallows to great advantage. In many instances a Bermuda sloop would be able to outrun British naval vessels because a square-rigged man-of-war was unable to sail closely to windward, whereas the sloop could turn upwind and disappear off into the distance.

Schooners were two-masted ships which shared the speed and manoeuvrability of the sloop, but with a narrower hull and a shallow draft of only 5 ft This was the ship developed for use along the American seaboard. The drawback was a slightly reduced cargo space, but as a hide-and-seek vessel she was superb.

The brigantines were larger – often 80 to 100 ft long and weighing between 125 and 150 tons, but unable to enter waters of less than 16 ft. This perhaps explains why fewer than ten per cent of attacks on Caribbean shipping in the period 1710 to 1730 involved pirate brigantines. A brigantine could not be easily hidden, nor could it slip past shoals and shallow sandbanks.

By the 1720s the word brigantine had evolved to refer to a type of rigging – the foremost of the two masts would be fully square-rigged and the mainmast would be rigged with both a fore- and aft-mainsail (known as a gaff sail). They would sometimes be supplemented by additional sails known as top gallants and royals. Brigantines were fast, and they could carry more than a hundred men. Typically, they would be armed with a dozen cannon, as well as swivel guns. The cannon would be used to fire a variety of items – from iron balls to gravel, and from grape-shot to nails. The actual choice would depend on the intended target, with the usual intention being to rip the sails and rigging to pieces so that the target was effectively disabled.

Apart from cannon, the pirates would have been able to use grenadoes – a sort of precursor to the hand grenade. Also called powder flasks, the grenado was usually made out of either iron or glass and had a spherical shape the size of a grapefruit;

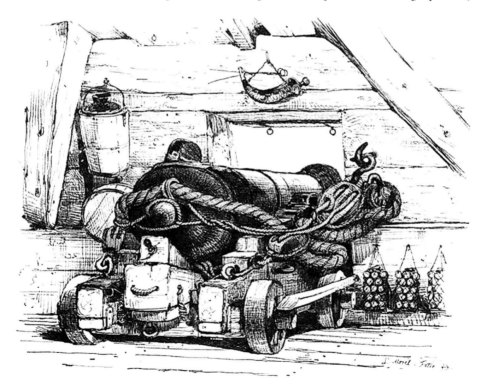

A 36-pounder cannon.

they had hollowed-out interiors which would be filled with gunpowder, grapeshot or shrapnel. Their fuse would be lit just before it was hurled at the ship being attacked, but they were somewhat unreliable weapons which could easily blow up in the face of the person using them. Some variants were designed to hurl noxious fumes onto the deck (when they would be known as stinkpots – designed to leave victims choking and blinded by the smoke and fumes).

So far as small arms were concerned the pirate had a veritable arsenal at his disposal – usually depending upon what he had been able to steal. The flintlock pistol was perhaps the favourite, but they were slow to load and hence the pirate would often go into battle with three or four already loaded and ready for use. Musketoons and blunderbusses were favoured for close-quarter fighting, while the musket (along with the good old bow and arrow) would be used as a sniping weapon to pick off targets before the actual attempt was made to board a victim. As far as hand weapons were concerned the double-edged sword was often used, but history suggests that the cutlass was the preferred weapon of choice. With a blade length of perhaps 24 inches it was easy to wield even in the confined areas on board ship.

In the shallow waters of the Caribbean the pirate ships could sail rings around a big man-of-war. They knew the shallows and the shoals, and used them to advantage, often cocking a snook at naval vessels which were unable to follow them. This was especially relevant in the harbour of New Providence Island, where in addition to the main harbour entrance to the west, there was a narrow eastern exit which could only be used by ships able to cross a low sand bar called Potters Cay. In practice this meant that the eastern route could only be used by ships with a draft of less than 8 ft – and this certainly excluded most ships of the Royal Navy.

To counter this, the navy needed smaller more agile ships, hence the push to build more sixth-rate ships, typically of between 450 and 550 tons. They would carry a crew of between 150 and 240 men, and would pack a significant punch with up to twenty-eight carriage-mounted guns. To begin with in the eighteenth century, these were usually firing six-pound cannon balls but in time the larger nine-pound balls were used. They were often referred to as frigates, and comprised a single-deck square-rigged vessel.

Typically, a naval frigate would have nineteen officers. Heading the list were the captain and two lieutenants. Warrant officers included the master, the ship's surgeon and the purser, and there would be others, the gunner, the bosun and the carpenter along with master's mates, the surgeon's assistant and so on. There would often be over twenty marines on board and in that case there would be a marine officer in charge. What was known as 'the lower deck' was made up of the rest of the crew, who had to make do with extremely cramped quarters, sleeping in hammocks hung within touching distance of each other.

During the reign of King William III the number of these smaller ships more than doubled from 49 in 1689 to 108 in 1702, but it was not until the reign of George I that the vessels were deployed expressly to police the seas in order to curb piracy. By 1718 there were a dozen ships stationed in the Caribbean or off the coast of North America, patrolling those areas. These included the *Ludlow Castle, Swift, Scarborough, Seaford, Pearle, Lyme,* and *Phoenix*, all of which were given orders to act in concert against the pirates. In the Caribbean, the Navy developed two separate naval bases where their ships could be provisioned, repaired and maintained – one at Port Royal in Jamaica, and the other at English Harbour on Antigua in the Leeward Islands. In each place, half a dozen frigates might be based. It subsequently transpired that while these harbours were ideally placed to carry out anti-piracy patrols, they were quite inadequate to mount major attacks on French and Spanish interests and when major wars erupted during the eighteenth century other temporary harbours and dock facilities had to be created.

Two aspects of life at sea need to be considered in connection with the way that the pirates operated, especially in the Caribbean. The first was their reaction to the prevailing sailors' practice of 'running down a westing' (or its converse, 'running down an easting'); and secondly the necessity of careening.

The first was a reflection of the fact that in the early part of the eighteenth century there was no reliable way of calculating longitude. Accurate sextants and lunar tables, along with the invention of a truly reliable and accurate marine chronometer by Harrison, had to wait until the latter part of the century. Difficulties in establishing longitude meant that sailors would often sail to the latitude of their destination, then turn towards where they wanted to go and thereafter follow a line of constant latitude. So, typically, if a merchant wanted to sail from Bristol to Jamaica in the West Indies he would first head down to Madeira in order to reach the correct latitude, and then sail due west for the Caribbean, Basically, it was easier to sail two sides of a triangle rather than to travel along the hypotenuse. One drawback to this 'lazy' way of navigating was that it meant that sailors often failed to make use of the prevailing currents or of favourable winds, resulting in the voyages being extended by days and even weeks. This in turn increased the likelihood of food and water running out, which could lead to poor health and even death for members of the crew. Scurvy and starvation were major killers on long sea voyages until well into the second half of the century.

However, running down a westing had the advantage that it minimised the risk of getting lost and overshooting the intended destination. On the other hand, it also meant that pirates could work out exactly what direction ships would be coming from. For instance, if a merchant was aiming for the plantations of Jamaica, all the pirates had to do was secrete their ships behind a suitable headland on the particular line of latitude on which Jamaica stands, and wait for their prey to fall into the trap. It greatly increased their chances, especially if local knowledge gleaned onshore already gave them a rough idea as to when shipping was expected.

This, then, is the background to Johnson's comments in the preface to *A General History* when he says:

> *Latitude is the only Certainty in those Voyages to be found, and then they sail due West, till they come to their Port, without altering their Course. In this West Way lye the pirates … so that if the Merchant Ships bound thither, do not fall a Prey to them one Day, they must another.*

Another factor worked to the advantage of the pirates – the predictability of the trade winds. Merchants had a strong economic reason to follow these winds – it is why they got the name 'trade winds'. However, it also meant that the pirates knew the routes being used, especially when the winds blew through narrow channels separating islands. This was why Tortuga, off the northern coast of modern-day Haiti, proved a popular base for piracy. There, ships could lie in wait, hidden from view, ready to pounce as merchantmen made their way up along the coast of Florida.

If knowledge of merchant shipping routes was a plus for the pirates, the need for careening was a definite minus. Careening was the name given to tipping a ship over onto its side in order to clean the hull and to remove barnacles, sea-weed etc. Nowadays this is generally done in a dry dock, but 300 years ago this was not an option. And oddly, it affected pirate ships far more than merchant ships, for the simple reason that speed was of the essence to the pirate. A smooth hull made for a fast ship. In the warm tropical waters of the Caribbean the growth in marine life over the hull was swift and inevitable. It meant that the ship was dragging a carpet of weed, as well as adding many hundredweight to the weight of the vessel, so numerous were the barnacles. In extreme cases this could result in the ship being slowed down to half her normal speed. That was a real problem if you were a pirate, relying on being able to 'hit and run'. Speed enabled the pirates to capture their prize, but speed could also get them out of trouble.

It was different for the merchantmen, where time was money. A week spent careening their ship meant a week when no profits were being made. It was therefore more tempting for the owner to put off careening until he got back to his home port. It was also far easier to careen a ship which was empty of cargo – whereas taking everything off the ship on some Caribbean island or other, and stacking the stores and cargo on shore, was just asking for trouble from pilferers.

So it was that every couple of months the pirate would head for some suitable spot, called a careenage, where the necessary work could be done, preferably away

Careening a vessel.

from prying eyes. The procedure left the pirates extremely vulnerable, and on at least one occasion a pirate was 'caught with his pants down'. In 1723 Captain George Lowther called in on the remote island of Blanquilla in order to careen his pirate ship *Revenge*. He was spotted by Walter Moore, in command of HMS *Eagle* and although Moore cornered him Lowther managed to escape and made it ashore to the island. Once there, he shot himself in the head rather than face being taken prisoner and tried for piracy.

Careening required a detailed knowledge of safe anchorages. Faced with a problem of a tidal difference of perhaps only 2 or 3 ft throughout the Caribbean, the correct careenage was vital. The captain needed a place where the water shelved off sharply close to the shore. Often this would be at the back of a sand bar or by islands in the mouths of rivers where a strong current operated as the tide went out. Great care was needed in positioning the ship. Blocks would be fastened to the masts and ropes and pulleys would then be used to pull the boat over onto its side as the water level dropped. The pirate needed a large rock or tree onshore to give enough leverage, and as the entire weight of the ship was resting on the widest part of the hull, it was sometimes necessary to pack the hull at both ends in order to spread the load.

Before this could happen, everything heavy or moveable had to be taken off the ship by longboat and stored onshore – all the guns, all the ballast, all the barrels of water and dried goods, everything. It was also necessary to caulk all the gunports correctly, using oakum and pitch, so that water was kept out from the beached vessel.

The crew could then set to work scraping off the barnacles and weed and assess whether timbers needed to be replaced. This could be a frequent occurrence in warm water, due to the spread of the seawater clam known as *teredo navalis*, or the common shipworm. This could cause a frightening amount of damage to ship's timbers, boring holes into the wood until it resembled a sponge.

Once the exposed side of the hull had been treated the ship would then be floated upright on the incoming tide, then turned round and re-positioned so that the crew could access the other side. Often the pirates would be unable to get hold of the white-lead paint favoured by the navy and used in merchant ships. They were also unlikely to have large quantities of the sulphur, tar, and tallow which was used to cover the white surface in order to try and keep the vessel watertight and to deter wood-boring animals. They were therefore faced with no alternative but to careen on a regular basis.

It was a frustrating and arduous business, and gave rise to the various references in Johnson's *A General History* to times when pirates had to 'stop to clean' every six weeks or so. Cleanliness was not so much next to godliness, as next to an absolute necessity. It meant that when the entire moveable contents of the ship would be stacked on shore, the crew would live on the island and generally enjoy drinking bouts – a sort of careening party – which could last for many days and nights. If they were lucky, the captain would have chosen a careenage where there was fresh water, fruit trees and game to shoot – a welcome chance to escape from the tedium of over-salted dried meat and stale food. If they were unlucky, they would find that the hull was so badly honeycombed with sea-worm that it would render the ship un-seaworthy, necessitating the need for supplies of suitable replacement timber. Small wonder that if the pirates subsequently encountered a merchant ship in better condition than their own, they simply transferred themselves onto the captured vessel and abandoned what would otherwise have been a floating coffin. It is worth remembering that Alexander Selkirk originally asked to be put ashore in the Juan Fernandez Islands because he was convinced that the hull of the ship *Cinque Ports* was un-seaworthy. There he remained for four-and-a-half years, unaware that his premonition was correct: the *Cinque Ports* sank shortly after Selkirk was abandoned, with the loss of all but a handful of those on board.

This then was the reality of careening, a messy, time-consuming task. On one occasion the pirate 'Black Sam' Bellamy tried to compel captured sailors to carry out the work for him, but they were unused to the task of barnacle-scraping and took twice as long to finish the job. It was a case of 'if you want a job doing quickly, do it yourself'.

Repairing sails – a regular shore-based activity for all pirate crews.

Part Three

THE FINAL PHASE OF THE GOLDEN AGE

Engraving showing the pirate Edward England. In the background, *Fancy* and *Cassandra* exchange broadsides.

Introduction

By 1700 the authorities on both sides of the Atlantic were getting increasingly concerned at the damage to trade caused by the burgeoning number of pirates. Estimates vary, but it has been suggested that there were over 3,000 individuals engaged in piracy down the eastern seaboard of the American colonies and throughout the Caribbean. That is 3,000 men all trying to disrupt trade to pursue their own ends, 3,000 criminals making life difficult for legitimate traders.

England was emerging as a major trading nation, and its merchants were having to bear heavy losses as their cargoes were stolen. Traders were constantly complaining that their ships, fully laden, were held up in port, unable to sail, because of fears that pirates were lying in wait for them. The ships therefore had to wait until they had the support of a convoy of other ships i.e., so that they had safety in numbers. If they were lucky they might get a warship as an escort, but waiting for these convoys to assemble took time, and therefore money.

Just as importantly, the country wanted to make sure that the colonies 'paid for themselves' – it was expensive for the Crown to have to defend the colonies, to build fortifications, to garrison troops, to pay for the administration of justice, build infrastructures and so on. This money had to come from taxation and of course piracy struck at the heart of the problem. The pirates paid no taxes on the goods they seized and subsequently sold on. They were in a sense part of the wider problem of smuggling, and the government were determined to do something about it.

Against this background the early years of the century saw a long and exhausting war in Europe, known as the War of the Spanish Succession. As already mentioned, this lasted from 1701 to 1713 and was really the first world war of modern times. It involved theatres of war in Spain, Italy, Germany, Holland – and at sea. Charles II, King of Spain, had died in 1700. He was an unfortunate soul – mentally and physically handicapped, with a distended jaw which prevented him chewing, and an oversized tongue which made it difficult for him to talk.

He died at the age of 39 without leaving any issue and in his Will he gave the Crown to the French prince Philip of Anjou, grandson of King Louis XIV. He went on to become Philip V – the first Bourbon monarch in Spain. This had the effect of totally upsetting the balance of power in Europe, and was opposed by the British, the Dutch and the Austrians.

Britain, in particular, did not want the French extending their interests in the Caribbean, or taking over the Spanish Empire overseas.

The conflict meant that for a dozen years English sailors had a regular employment, either in the Royal Navy itself, or with the privateers operating their own ships under a Letter of Marque. Pay may not have been good, conditions may have been hard, but it was a living, and one to which they had become accustomed. Then, suddenly, 'the gravy train' stopped. The Treaty of Utrecht in 1713 had the effect of throwing the sailors out of work – and in those days there was no provision for half-pay, or social welfare for the unemployed. The money simply dried up, throwing thousands of men onto the scrapheap. Small wonder that for many, they simply made the transition from privateer to pirate, doing exactly what they had been doing for the past twelve years, but this time doing it for themselves.

The Caribbean had become a festering sore, with starving, desperate sailors causing all sorts of problems for the authorities. Port Royal in Jamaica had always been a popular piracy stronghold, but in time the Brethren preferred to base themselves on Tortuga, where there was no effective government, and on the almost lawless islands of the Bahamas, particularly New Providence Island. A succession of corrupt governors, lack of investment in infrastructure, and a tiny indigenous population meant that the pirates were able to establish a base in the Bahamas without significant opposition. Jamaica still had its problems, with Sir Nicholas Lawes, who was based on the island, writing to the Council of Trade and Plantations in August 1717, saying:

Many depredations have been committed by pirates of all nations who infest those seas; and are so powerfull, that the merchants ships have been, and are obliged to stay after their being loaded till one of H.M. ships of war could or can see them out of the danger of them; to the great loss of traders, owners of vessels, and H.M. Revenue.

The problem was that there were not enough naval protection vessels to go round, and it took time for the British Government to commission the right type of ship for the purpose. The pirate ships were small and fleet, they could hide in bays and escape through shallow waters. There was no way that a lumbering warship could follow its elusive prey into those shallows. What was needed were far more, but also far smaller, naval patrol ships.

British warships were rated from the largest, the first-rate, down to the smallest, the sixth-rate. As has been seen, the reign of King William saw a near doubling in the numbers of the smaller sixth-raters being commissioned. It took time for these ships to be used effectively against the pirates, and as a result piracy enjoyed a final flourish in the period between 1713 and 1730, before the murderous trade was finally brought to a halt. It is against this background that it is useful to look at the exploits of some of the individual pirates who made their name during this final flourish. Much of the information about their lives comes from the *General History of Pyrates* mentioned earlier, but it is worth looking behind some of the romanticised myths in order to ask the question: just how successful were they?

Chapter 9

The Great Storm of 1715: Biographies of Jennings, Hornigold and Bellamy and England

If any one event acted as a catalyst for the expansion of piracy in its final, golden, phase, it was the hurricane which hit the coast of Florida in 1715. For years, during the War of Spanish Succession, the annual treasure ships had been unable to sail across the Atlantic for fear of being captured by enemy war ships. Spanish coffers were empty and the country was facing bankruptcy. The Spanish king urgently needed the treasure shipments to be resumed so he sent a small fleet of eleven ships from Spain to Mexico to load the gold and silver, which was stored in warehouses waiting to be transported, and ordered the fleet to return as soon as possible. That was in 1712 but, for a variety of unforeseen reasons, there was a delay of two and a half years before the fleet was ready to return, by which time the king was desperate.

The ships included five carrying treasure from Mexico, and another seven from South America including bullion from the gold mines of Peru. There was a twelfth ship in the convoy, not directly linked to the treasure shipment, a French-owned frigate called the *Grifon* – heading for France but happy to use the galleons and their escorts as protection on its homeward journey. The convoy was under the overall command of Captain-General Don Juan Esteban de Ubilla, while General Don Antonio de Echeverz y Zubuza had particular responsibility for the South American ships. In total they were carrying an official cargo of 7 million pieces of eight, but unrecorded cargo may have made the value very much higher than this. It was not uncommon for unregistered cargo to be thirty, forty or fifty per cent more than registered cargo upon which tax had been paid. Indeed, the mine owners, who had been unable to sell the bullion for several years, may well have had cash-flow problems and under-declared the value of the cargo to a very significant degree.

On 24 July 1715 the twelve ships, which had assembled at Havana in Cuba, set off for Spain. It was late in the season, and the captain-general would have known that the hurricane season was imminent. He made haste up the narrow channel running up through the Florida Straits, intending then to head north of Bermuda before crossing the Atlantic. Six days into the voyage the convoy was in the region of Cape Canaveral; it became hot and oppressive and as the day progressed the skies darkened and the fleet was lashed with rain. The seas became mountainous as the full force of the hurricane hit. Miguel de Lima y Melo, in charge of the *Urca de Lima*, later described events:

> *The sun disappeared and the wind increased in velocity coming from the east and east northeast. The seas became very giant in size, the wind continued blowing us toward shore, pushing us into shallow water. It soon happened that we were unable to use any sail at all, making bare our yards, mostly due to the wind carrying away our sails and rigging, and we were at the mercy of the wind and water, always driven closer to the shore. Having then lost all of our masts, all of the ships wrecked on the shore, and with the exception of mine, broke to pieces. We lost only thirty seamen and marines, who were carried away by waves while in the waist of the ship.*

The hurricane reached a crescendo in the early hours of the morning on 31 July. Writing a fortnight later, one of the survivors, Father Francisco de León y Cabrera, described the events of that night:

> *The hurricane was so severe and turbulent … [experienced sailors] had never seen one like it. Such was the violence of the sea waves that they seemed like arrows even to those on land, so that many who managed to reach the shore also were killed. It is calculated that more than 600 other persons drowned or were missing from all the ships in these coasts and beaches, with the added misfortune that, after some of the ships and part of the cargo of others had been washed ashore, the furious swaying to and fro of the sea waves would drag everything back into the ocean, where it disappeared so that the coast was bare again.*

The only ship to have escaped unscathed was the *Grifon*, whose captain had chosen a more easterly course, further out from land. Unaware of the tragedy, he carried on alone across the Atlantic to Le Havre, not knowing that 1,000 men had perished. Those that were spared drowning succumbed to starvation, dehydration and wounds. The entire treasure, equivalent to tens of millions of pounds, either lay at the bottom of the sea or was scattered over the shoals and shallows which are a hallmark of the Florida coast.

The nearest Spanish settlement on the mainland of Florida was at San Augustin over 130 miles away. A longboat was dispatched with an urgent request for assistance. Meanwhile the survivors, now under the command of Admiral Salmón, gathered together and constructed a fortified shelter. Another ship's boat retraced the 360-mile journey back to Havana with an urgent request for supplies – and for divers to help recover as much as possible of the treasure.

The divers must have had a miserable job. They consisted of slaves and native Indians – and there are believed to have been some 300 of them. Each would be forced to jump into the shark-infested waters carrying a rock to help him submerge, and he was then expected to gather up coins and anything of value and bring them back to the surface. Divers were required to attach ropes to larger items of value, so that these could then be hauled to the surface. Working in up to 15 metres of water, the divers were at risk of getting the bends, and it is reported that over a third of the divers perished in this way. Nevertheless, large quantities of treasure were recovered and sent back to Havana. Further gold and silver was stored at the site of the salvage camp pending transfer.

Not surprisingly, news of the disaster, and of the recovery operation, spread like wildfire once the treasure started to arrive back in Cuba. From San Augustin news of the events further south reached Boston, and was promptly reported on in the *Boston News-letter*, a newspaper read by the English colonists, and circulated (over time) throughout many of the English settlements down as far as the Bahamas. The *Boston News-Letter* had started over ten years earlier, and had built up a reputation as being 'published by authority' – carrying news of official business from England such as proclamations and so on, supplemented by snippets of news brought in by visiting ship's captains. The report of a massive bullion shipment lying just off the Florida Coast caused a sensation; the gold rush was well and truly on.

The stories of many of the pirates who flourished during this period became entwined as they rushed to the scene – men such as Henry Jennings, Samuel Bellamy, Benjamin Hornigold and Edward England – and although their stories often overlap, they can be looked at in turn.

Henry Jennings

First to arrive off the Florida coast was Henry Jennings on the 40-ton sloop *Barsheba*. The vessel carried eight guns and would normally have a crew of eighty. Jennings had been living on Jamaica when the news of the wreck, and of the huge salvage operation, came through in early November 1715. He obtained a commission from the governor of the island, a man by the name of Lord Archibald Hamilton, to 'execute all manner of Acts of Hostility against pyrates according to the Law of Arms', but the commission went on to expressly state that Jennings was not to attack anyone except pirates. It is worth remembering that the Spanish had not abandoned the site, and Spain and Britain were no longer at war. There is also a strong suspicion that the governor in fact helped finance the trip, buying shares in the venture, and informed Jennings unofficially that he was free to attack the Spanish guarding the wrecks and to retrieve as much of the treasure as they could lay their hands on. Jennings took with him fourteen divers, and was accompanied by Captain John Wills in command of the *Eagle*.

On Christmas Day, Jennings encountered a Spanish mail ship carrying mail from San Augustin bound for Havana. The vessel, captained by Pedro de la Vega, was searched, but not very thoroughly or they would have discovered that she was carrying 1,200 gold pieces of eight. Instead they got information from the captain as to the exact whereabouts of the wrecked treasure ship *Urca de Lima*, as well as the fact that any recovered treasure was kept by the Spanish at the lightly-guarded salvage camp. Not for Jennings the wearisome task of trying to locate and bring up treasure from the seabed. He took the much easier option of stealing what had already been recovered, sending ashore a party of some 300 men under cover of darkness. They heavily outnumbered the camp's defenders, and quickly overran the camp. The Spanish salvage team were still under the command of Admiral Salmón. He surrendered, and Jennings and Wills seized treasure with a face value of £87,000 – a massive fortune, equivalent nowadays to nearly £9 million. Off they sailed to New Providence Island, after first releasing Pedro de la Vega and his mail ship.

Arriving at New Providence Island they stayed long enough to have a few nights of drunken revelry – and long enough too to realise that the overcrowding on the *Barsheba* would be much assisted by an additional vessel, which Jennings forcibly took from Benjamin Hornigold. The portion of treasure due to the crew was divided up and distributed, and the small squadron then sailed back to Jamaica, with 120,000 pieces of eight on board. En route to Jamaica they captured and plundered a Spanish merchant ship, but they allowed the ship to continue its journey to Cuba. When it arrived, it brought news of the plunder and theft to the Viceroy. He was absolutely furious at the outrage, and immediately threatened to string up any Englishmen he came across unless Hamilton hanged Jennings and his men. Hamilton did no such thing, and chaired the Vice-Admiralty Court which adjudicated on the prize which Jennings had brought back.

Jennings was regarded as a hero on Jamaica, but it was a dangerous place for him to be, given that the Spanish had dispatched three ships to try and capture him and bring him to justice. It was inadvisable for him to stay on the island so, early in 1716, he sailed back on the *Barsheba*, to try and seize more treasure from the salvors. This time they offered him 25,000 pieces of eight to leave them alone. He took the money but still carried on pillaging. He also stopped and plundered a Jamaican merchant ship, with an English crew and under an English captain, and when news of that act of piracy reached Jamaican ears, Governor Hamilton was none-too-pleased.

Jennings continued to attack shipping – often bringing himself into conflict with his opposite number Hornigold, because they frequently found themselves chasing the same prize. When Hornigold seized a French merchant ship Jennings appeared on the scene and took it away from under his nose. Later in April 1716 Jennings captured another French vessel called the *Sainte Marie* together with a cargo of bullion. Two ships loyal to Hornigold, under the command of Bellamy and Williams, double-crossed Jennings and 'liberated' 28,500 pieces of eight from the captured *Sainte Marie*. On another occasion Hornigold tried to 'assist' in the capture of the *Marianne* and was sent away with an ultimatum not to interfere in 'official business'.

By the end of April 1716 Jennings had moved to a new base in the Bahamas, where the pirate population had swelled to over 1,000 men, many of them following Jennings from Jamaica. There had been a total breakdown in any form of government on New Providence Island, leaving the pirates free to do as they wished. In effect they split into two factions, one dominated by Jennings and the other by his rival Hornigold. The hostility between the two men was considerable, with Jennings enjoying the support of men such as Vane and Rackham, while Hornigold was supported by Edward Teach, Stede Bonnet and Samuel Bellamy. They may have described themselves collectively as 'the Flying Gang', or even as 'the Pirate Republic', but it was in fact a society built only on fear, criminality and self-interest.

Back on Jamaica the days of Governor Hamilton were numbered, and in the autumn of 1716 he was arrested for violating Anglo–Spanish peace treaties and was recalled to Britain. Ironically the ship he sailed on was captured by Jennings, but the captors seemed more interested in helping themselves to the twenty gallons of rum which they found on board, rather than in taking the private belongings of the ex-Governor. Hamilton was forced to complete his journey home on board HMS *Bedford*.

Jennings continued plundering, but when he heard that George I was offering a free pardon to any pirates prepared to hand themselves in and to renounce piracy, Jennings sailed to Bermuda in early 1718 with fifteen of his crew to surrender to the authorities. He became one of perhaps 400 pirates to take advantage of the King's Pardon – and also one of the very few who retired from his 'profession' and enjoyed a lengthy and wealthy retirement as a plantation owner on Bermuda. He is, however, believed to have obtained a Letter of Marque in 1745 at the start of the War of Austrian Succession. By then he would have been in his sixties, and one version of events has him captured by a Spanish ship, imprisoned, and dying in captivity. The truth is impossible to ascertain.

Benjamin Hornigold

Hornigold was one of the many privateers who turned to piracy after the end of the War of Spanish Succession in 1714. Born in England in around 1680, possibly in Norfolk, he established his reputation as a privateer based on the island of Jamaica. Later, after George I came to the British throne, he helped establish New Providence Island as the main pirate base in the Caribbean.

It was an ideal base, with its myriad of cays and islets offering a secure and hidden anchorage, close to the main shipping lane used by trans-Atlantic vessels. By July 1716 Governor Alexander Spotswood was already aware of Hornigold, writing to the Council of Trade and Plantations with the deposition of a man called John Vickers:

In Nov. last Benjamin Hornigold arrived at Providence in the sloop Mary of Jamaica, belonging to Augustine Golding, which Hornigold took upon the Spanish coast, and soon after the taking of the said sloop, he took a Spanish sloop loaded with dry goods and sugar, which cargo he disposed of at Providence, but the Spanish sloop was taken from him by Capt. Jennings of the sloop Bathsheba [sic] of Jamaica. In January Hornigold sailed from Providence in the said sloop Mary, having on board 140 men, 6 guns and 8 pattararas [swivel guns], and soon after returned with another Spanish sloop, which he took on the coast of Florida. After he had fitted the said sloop at Providence, he sent Golding's sloop back to Jamaica to be returned to the owners: and in March last sailed from Providence in the said Spanish sloop, having on board near 200 men, but whither bound deponent knoweth not.

Thomas Walker was the acting Deputy Governor of the Bahamas and found himself totally unable to cope with the influx of criminals, writing in 1716:

I was formerly directed by H.E. Genll. Nicholson to render to your Lordships an accot. of the state and condition of ye Bohamia Islands wch. has a long time bin without governmts., The want of wch. has laid those Islands open to be a recepticall and shelter of pirates and loose fellows and gives ye inhabitants as well as ye trading vessuals from other parts ye liberty and oppertunity of inriching themselves by sideing and dealing with, entertaining and releiveing such villains who from time to time resort there to sell and dispose of their piraticall goods, and perfusely spend wtt.[what] they take from ye English, French and mostly Spaniards, and as I am an inhabitant of New Providence have bin an eye witness to those ellegiall and unwarrantable practises commited both by ye piratts and inhabitants and others tradeing there, and have used ye uttmost of my endeavours to put by and prevent them, as alsoe by my goeing to the Havana hath bin a means of preventing ye design of ye provoked Spaniards comeing to cut those Islands off for the piraces ytt. has since ye peace bin commited even by some of the inhabitants of those Islands.

   The pirates daly increse to Providence and haveing began to mount ye guns in ye Fort for there[their] defence and seeking ye oppertunity to kill mee because I was against their illegall and unwarrantable practices and by no means would consent to their mounting of guns in ye Fort upon such accots. I was thereupon forced with my wife and family to acquitt ye Island to my great expence and damage and ye latter part of June last arrived safe to this Province [South Carolina] where I remaine upon expence in hopes thatt H.M.[His Majesty] will be gratiously pleased to take those Islands under his care and protection, etc. that ye Islands may become a flourishing plantation, etc.

Hornigold used a number of vessels during his brief career as a pirate. Originally he had sailed in the *Happy Return*, a sloop owned by Jonathan Darvell, but Hornigold was unhappy with the division of the profits and bought his own ship, and used it to capture two Cuban merchant ships carrying 46,000 pieces of eight. In 1715 he captured a sloop which he renamed *Benjamin* with a crew of 200.

At some stage Hornigold's ship was a formidable sloop named *Ranger*, armed with thirty guns, but arguably his heart was not really in piracy – he refused to attack British ships, and he was too democratic to be a ruthless leader. He is however important in pirate lore because he mentored Edward Teach, appointing him as First Mate and in due course putting him in charge of his own vessel. As Blackbeard, Teach went on to far surpass his mentor in terms of fame and fortune. In his early days, Hornigold also took Sam Bellamy under his wing.

As a businessman, Hornigold was helped greatly by his association with John Cockram, who had moved to Harbour Island, 50 miles north of Nassau. Here he became the lynch-pin of the organisation needed by men such as Hornigold, both in terms of 'money laundering' (i.e., fencing stolen goods), supplying provisions and so on. It is probable that Hornigold bought some of his first ships (sailing canoes and sloops) from Cockram's supply chain. Cockram went on to marry the daughter of a local merchant, and developed a thriving business.

Towards the end of 1716 Hornigold combined forces with a number of other pirates, after promoting Bellamy to be in charge of the *Marianne*. Together they linked up with the French pirate Olivier La Buse and became a real menace to shipping in the area. They captured no fewer than forty-two vessels in the six-month period up to March 1717. On one occasion Hornigold captured a merchant ship bound for Cuba carrying 120 barrels of flour, and on another he seized a Portuguese ship carrying wine from Madeira. These successes caused the Governor of South Carolina to send a heavily armed ship to hunt down Hornigold and his companions, but Hornigold turned the tables on his pursuer, forcing the crew to abandon their ship after running it aground at Cat's Quay, off the coast of Florida.

At that point it was reported that Hornigold was in charge of some 300 men, based on five ships. But when his merry band seized a sloop off the coast of Honduras one of the sloop's crew bizarrely reported that, 'They did us no further injury than the taking most of our hats from us, having got drunk the night before, as they told us, and toss'd theirs overboard.'

He lost his command after his men voted to lift the embargo on attacking English ships, and Bellamy took over as captain. Hornigold was left with a sloop named *Adventure*, with a small crew of twenty-six. When the opportunity to take the King's Pardon came up, Hornigold leapt at the opportunity and sailed to Jamaica to surrender. He then became an enthusiastic bounty hunter, chasing after some of his former allies. He particularly tried to track down Stede Bonnet and Calico Jack Rackham but without success. He did however capture a dozen pirates including John Augur, bringing them back to the newly arrived Governor Woodes Rogers for punishment. As already described, the prisoners were hanged at New Providence Island in early December 1718. Shortly after, Rogers wrote: 'I am glad of this new proof that Capt'n Hornigold has given to the world to wipe off the infamous name he has hither been known by Though he has admitted most people spoke well of his generosity.'

Finally, towards the end of 1719 it appears that fate caught up with Hornigold. One report suggested that he was captured by a Spanish vessel and died in captivity. Another, perhaps more likely report, claimed that he was caught in a hurricane at some unrecorded point between the Bahamas and the coast of Mexico. Johnson, in his *A General History*, simply states that he 'was cast away upon rocks, a great way from land, and perished…'. His ship, with almost all on board, was lost. Death at sea, as opposed to death at the end of a rope, was to prove an all-too-common end for the golden generation of pirates.

Samuel Bellamy ('Black Sam', aka 'Prince of Pirates', aka 'Robin Hood of the Seas')

Given the moniker 'Black Sam' because of his dark hair and swarthy complexion, Samuel Bellamy had been born in the central Devon village of Hittisleigh in February 1689. His mother died shortly after giving birth. In his teens he became a sailor in the Royal Navy, and by 1715 found himself in the Cape Cod area of Massachusetts. Here he is rumoured to have fallen in love with a girl called Mary Hallett, who may or may not have become pregnant by him, and whose parents may or may not have disapproved of her having anything to do with an impecunious young sailor. Equally she may already have been married. She may have been extremely young – or indeed extremely old. One story suggests that she enjoyed a witch-like reputation as a weird old lady shouting imprecations to the winds, bringing storms down around the ears of anyone who annoyed her. Whatever the truth, young Sam decided to go to sea to make his fortune, intending to come back and take Mary away.

In this endeavour he was greatly helped by his friendship with Paulsgrave Williams, by then a married man of 38 with children. Williams was a gold and silversmith whose father was Rhode Island Attorney General. Despite these wealthy connections he decided to leave his family and share a life at sea with Bellamy, and indeed helped fund his expedition. Together they went off intending to 'fish the wrecks' following the destruction of the Spanish treasure fleet. In all probability they arrived too late – the easy pickings had already gone and others were already on the scene. In practice, they met up with Hornigold who, as already mentioned, recognised Bellamy's skills as a sailor and put him in charge of the *Marianne*. They embarked on a life of piracy, capturing a small vessel called the *Sultana*, which Bellamy then used as his flagship, handing over control of the *Marianne* to Paulsgrave Williams. Bellamy and Williams acted in a particularly successful partnership. Having two vessels acting together made for an extremely effective unit and together they successfully pursued their chosen profession off Mexico's Yucatan Peninsula, retreating from time-to-time to their lair in the Virgin Islands. Between 1716 and 1717 Bellamy operated out of Blanco Islet (subsequently renamed Bellamy Cay) and from Trellis Bay on Beef Island, off the east coast of Tortola.

Then, in February 1717, something happened which catapulted Bellamy from the ranks of ordinary pirates, and which was to make him into one of the wealthiest men alive: he captured the *Whydah* galley. The *Whydah* was a state-of-the-art square-rigged three-masted ship on her maiden voyage. She had been built for speed (she could manage fifteen knots) and had been launched in London the year before. She had already completed the first two legs of the 'golden triangle' – exporting goods to Africa, picking up a cargo of slaves and selling them in the West Indies - and was now carrying a rich cargo back to Britain. The *Whydah* belonged to Sir Humphry Morice, a man who later became Governor of the Bank of England. He was a Member of Parliament – and one of the leading slave traders of the time. As it turned out, he was also a swindler and an embezzler who defrauded the Bank of England out of tens of thousands of pounds.

Five hundred slaves had made the journey on board the *Whydah*, and by the time this human cargo had been converted to cash, and the *Whydah* loaded with West Indian merchandise, she was a floating fortune. The *Whydah* may have been fitted with eighteen six-pounders, but when Bellamy caught sight of her in the Windward Passage, separating Hispaniola and Cuba, he was able to hunt her down over a period of three days. Eventually Captain Price, in charge of the *Whydah* and in his day a man who had served with Henry Morgan, surrendered to Bellamy with hardly a shot being fired. Price was rewarded with £20 in gold dust – and given the *Sultana* in exchange for the *Whydah*, and sent on his way.

Bellamy then stripped out all the unnecessary ships fittings, jettisoning the slave cages, removing much of the superstructure on deck including the pilot's cabin and captain's quarters, and added a further ten cannon. Here was a formidable fighting machine and on it Bellamy set sail for the Carolinas, looting ships along the way. But success was short-lived – after two months he and Williams decided to split up. Bellamy headed for a possible reunion with his girlfriend Mary Hallett, with an understanding that the pirates would reconvene off Block Island. On 26 April, Bellamy had encountered and captured the *Mary Anne*, a Boston sloop with a hold full of Madeira wine. According to the Gazette, which carried news of the event some five months afterwards, 'the pirates then entertained themselves so plentifully with the Madeira wine that they all got drunk.' A thick bank of fog settled over the sea, obliterating all visibility, meaning that the *Whydah* lost contact with the accompanying vessels *Anne* and *Fisher*. These two chose to set a course further out to sea, while Bellamy chose a course taking him dangerously close to the shore.

A strong North-easterly wind blew up and in the gale which followed, the *Whydah* was blown onto a sand bar off what is now Marconi Beach at Wellfleet, Massachusetts. During that night the main mast snapped and the vessel capsized after being dragged onto the shoals, scattering men and treasure across a four-mile stretch of coast. The extra cannon being carried on board smashed through the ship's timbers causing the *Whydah* to disintegrate in a remarkably short time. Over 100 men drowned immediately, including Bellamy. A survivor on board the *Whydah*, Thomas Davis, subsequently reported that, 'In a quarter of an hour after the ship struck, the Mainmast was carried by the board, and in the Morning she was beat to pieces.'

The Gazette of 24 September 1717 incorrectly described the *Whydah* as the *Widow*, and reported the incident with the words:

> On board of her were 120 Men, of whom only two were saved. The Man and Boy in the Ship which had been taken, seeing the seven Pirates who were put on board her drunk and asleep on the Decks, took that Opportunity to stand in for the Land, and ran her fast aground. The Pirates were secured by the Inhabitants, and carried to Boston.

The *Mary Anne* was also caught in the storm and wrecked. One of her survivors gave evidence that the *Whydah* had been carrying between 4.5 and 5 tons of gold and silver treasure, along with jewels and other valuables. The spoils had already been prepared for division among the crew, with 180 sacks of bullion each weighing 50 lbs – all of them scattered across the sea-bed. Although some attempts were made by groups from the shore to locate and retrieve the treasure, nothing of any significance was recovered. The handful of surviving pirates was rounded up and sent for trial in Boston on 18 October 1717, on charges of piracy and robbery. Six were found guilty and hanged. The two ship's carpenters faced a separate trial, where their defence (namely that they had been conscripted and forced into piracy against their will) was accepted and they were released.

A seventh man, a young Miskito Indian called John Julian who had been the pilot on board the *Whydah*, was spared a trial and instead was sold into slavery. He had a violent temperament, eventually escaped from his owner, and then killed the bounty hunter who had attempted to capture him. For that he was hanged on 26 March 1733, some sixteen years after the destruction of the *Whydah*.

While Bellamy was unsuccessfully battling the elements, his partner Williams was left waiting for a fortnight, unaware that he would not see his friend ever again. The arrangement with Bellamy was that they would meet up at Damariscove Island, and when it became apparent that Bellamy would not be coming, Williams was left with a quandary, as he was not a sailor by background. But, despite his prosperous heritage, Williams was so taken with the life of piracy that he decided to carry on.

An added problem for Williams, and his crew of twenty-eight, was that their share of the treasure had been placed on board the *Whydah*. No one would have wanted to leave the scene while there was a possibility of being reunited with their share. Reports suggest that after a fortnight Williams visited the area where Bellamy was wrecked but realised that nothing could be done. He departed the Cape Cod area, sailed south, and attacked a couple of vessels in Vineyard Sound. By 10 May the Boston News-Letter was reporting that:

On Wednesday last our Government fitted out two good sloops, well Arm'd and Man'd, under the Command of Col. John Cranston, and Captain Job Almy, in order to speak with a Pirate Sloop lurking on our Coast, commanded by Paul Williams.

There are reports that Williams stayed in the area, with the *Boston News-Letter* carrying a report that he was still raiding small vessels as late as June 1717:

Brown, in a sloop from South Carolina, who was taken ... by Paul Williams the Pirate, who took from him 350 ounces of silver, which was buried in his Ballast, for hiding it ... the Pirates threaten'd to burn his sloop.

Documentary records of what happened next are absent; one story suggests that he took advantage of the King's Pardon on 5 September 1717 and retired from piracy, at least for some years. Quite possibly he moved to the Nassau area and there are records suggesting that he was based in Nassau in 1718, possibly in some ancillary capacity (i.e., supplying goods to other pirates), when HMS *Phoenix* visited the island. If so, it is possible that Williams returned to his piratical ways after a few years, because there were reports that he was operating off the coast of Africa with the Frenchman Olivier La Buse throughout the year 1720. The same reports suggest that he finally retired at the age of 45 in 1723.

Over the years, Samuel Bellamy's name receded into the background, and Williams, his quartermaster, has become a mere footnote. The vast amount of treasure, resulting from not even two full years of piracy, was not really appreciated until the wreck of the *Whydah* was located in 1984. Details of the resulting treasure hunt are set out in Chapter 13, and *Whydah* remains the only fully authenticated pirate ship from the Golden Age of Piracy ever recovered. The items recovered show that Bellamy died an exceptionally wealthy man – someone described by *Forbes Magazine* as having accumulated the modern equivalent of £120 million – possibly more than any other pirate in history.

Edward England

Born Edward Seeger in Ireland in or around 1685, this most gentlemanly of pirates adopted the name of Edward England when his piracy got under way in 1717. Before then, he had served as a privateer off Jamaica but was captured by Christopher Winter and given the option of joining his crew.

England was part of Jennings's small fleet which descended on the Florida coast after the storm of 1715, looting the Spanish salvage camp and escaping with salvaged gold with a value of £87,000. England then served as quartermaster to Captain Vane on board the *Lark*, but in March 1718 the *Lark* was captured by a Royal Navy ship and England was released in an attempt to induce others to accept the King's Pardon. In practice neither Vane nor England took up the offer of pardon from Woodes Rogers. Instead, both moved their operations away from the Bahamas and over to the West coast of Africa, where they spent the next year pillaging and stealing. Captive vessels included the *Cadogan*, under the command of a man called Skinner. He was known to some of England's crew as a man who owed them wages; they accordingly tied him up, threw bottles at him from close range, and then shot him through the head with a flintlock pistol. That left a vacancy on the *Cadogan*, filled by England when he appointed a young Howell Davis to act as captain. Davis went on to be a feared and successful pirate – and one who was to take Bartholomew Roberts and a number of other young pirates under his wing.

England succeeded in capturing the *Pearl*, a frigate, renaming her the *Royal James* and on it he sailed down towards the Cape, seizing around a dozen ships along the way. He also found time to fall out with the local populace in one of the coastal towns, so he burned it to the ground. Having rounded the Cape, England moved up the coast into the Indian Ocean where he joined forces with the French pirate Olivier Levasseur, otherwise known as La Buse. Together they enjoyed considerable success. In 1720 England captured a Dutch ship, carrying thirty-four guns and a large cargo, and he decided to make this his flagship, renaming her the *Fancy* in honour of Henry Avery who had gained such success in the area twenty years earlier.

The *Fancy* then encountered a ship belonging to the East India Company, called the *Cassandra*. She was under the command of Captain McRae and was carrying a cargo stated to be worth £75,000. The two ships joined in battle off the Comoros Islands, and after a lengthy encounter both ships were heavily damaged, especially the *Fancy*. Eventually McRae surrendered to England, who declined to torture his prisoner and indeed suggested that they simply swap ships and go their separate ways. England's crew resented this – not for them the idea that they should spare the lives of English prisoners. There was a mutiny, England was deposed as captain and along with three other men was marooned on an uninhabited island with next-to-no provisions.

According to *A General History*, one of the men marooned alongside England was a 'a man with a terrible pair of whiskers and a wooden leg, being stuck round with pistols' – and some have argued that he became the inspiration for Long John Silver.

The quartet scavenged what food they could, and constructed a rough boat on which they escaped their island prison after nearly four months. They sailed to St Augustine's Bay in Madagascar, a pirate settlement, and appear to have been given assistance and food by the local pirates. England succumbed to a tropical disease and died sometime in 1720/21. Johnson, in his *A General History*, leaves us with this eulogy:

> *He had a great deal of good Nature, and did not want for Courage; he was not avaritious, and always averse to the ill Usage of Prisoners received: He would have been contented with moderate Plunder, and less mischievous Pranks, could his Companions have been brought to the same Temper, but he was generally over-rul'd, and as he was engaged in that abominable Society, he was obliged to be a Partner in all their vile Actions.*

Eighteenth Century woodcut of Edward 'Ned' England.

Chapter 10

A Short Rope or a Long Drop: Biographies of Charles Vane, Stede Bonnet, William Fly and Olivier Levasseur

Charles Vane

Charles Vane would have been 37 when his ship accompanied Henry Jennings on his 1717 raid of the salvor's camp off Florida. Four years later Vane was dead, echoing the story of the many hundreds of pirates who paid the price for rejecting the terms

An early eighteenth-century woodcut of Charles Vane.

of the King's Pardon. But his time as a pirate showed a glorious defiance, and for that reason he was an influential figure, especially in the autumn of 1717 when he was based in the Bahamas. The many hundreds of pirates infesting the island had split into two camps and the one favouring outright opposition to the authority of King George was led by Charles Vane. He may well have had Jacobite sympathies, and the stories of toasts being drunk to 'King James III' may be indicative of this. Equally, it may have simply been a reflection of a more general feeling of 'King George can go and get stuffed – we don't need him.' This is borne out by a report that Vane was actually opposed to any form of external government, Protestant or Catholic.

Vane started a cat-and-mouse game with British authorities when in February 1718 Captain Pearse arrived off New Providence Island on board the *Phoenix*. Vane's sloop *Lark* was captured, but in an effort to encourage the pirate community to accept the pardon, Pearse released Vane, but kept the *Lark*. Unfortunately, this had the opposite effect to the one intended. Vane and his supporters, who at that stage included Rackham and England, resumed their piratical ways and in March seized a sloop operating out of Jamaica. Vane brazenly returned to taunt and provoke Pearse.

The *Phoenix* was in the deep water on the western side of the harbour, so Vane brought the captured sloop into harbour from the eastern side, knowing that the shoal separating the two halves of the harbour was too shallow for Pearse to cross. Pearse had to watch helplessly as Vane plundered and unloaded the captured sloop right in front of him, and then suffer the humiliation of listening to the sounds of Vane and his men carousing into the early hours of the morning. To make the humiliation even greater, when Pearse sent some of his men, armed with muskets, in a longboat in an attempt to surprise the pirates, the man on watch spotted their approach and raised the alarm. The men in the longboat were forced to retreat as they no longer had the element of surprise. Suddenly the Royal Navy no longer looked a mighty power – Vane was demonstrating that his own power was even greater. He even managed to retake the *Lark* from under Pearse's nose, and persuaded three of Pearse's men to defect to the pirate's cause. By early April 1718 Pearse departed the island, leaving it to be lorded over by the triumphant Vane.

The *Lark* was renamed *Ranger*, and on it Vane carried out a number of highly successful raids, gaining a reputation as a cruel man who did not hesitate to torture his captives in order to speed up the process of discovering any items of value on board the ships which he had taken. In the early summer of 1718 he seized nine ships, making up an impressive flotilla which he intended to bring back to New Providence. Johnson, in his *A General History*, says that Vane:

> had the impudence to come ashore with his sword in hand, threaten to burn the
> principal houses of the town, and to make examples of many of the people; and

though he committed no murders, his behaviour was extremely insolent to all who were not as great villains as himself. He reigned here as Governor 20 days, stopped all vessels which came in, and would suffer none to go out. Being informed of a Governor being sent from England, he swore, while he was in the harbour, he would suffer no other Governor there himself.

Among the ships Vane captured was a French vessel armed with twenty guns, which Vane had in mind to make his flagship. As has been mentioned, he sailed her back into the harbour on New Providence just before the new governor, Woodes Rogers, was due to arrive on the island. When Rogers sailed towards the harbour he managed to get Vane boxed in, but Vane responded by loading the French ship with powder, setting her alight and leaving her to drift towards the English fleet. In the confusion which followed, Rogers had to manoeuvre his ships out of the way, effectively removing the blockade and leaving Vane simply to sail past them. It was a salutary lesson for Woodes Rogers, whose exploits have been dealt with more fully in chapter 7.

Vane went up to Charles Town and seized a number of valuable cargoes and so infuriated the authorities there that they commissioned Colonel Rhett (mentioned subsequently in connection with the capture of Stede Bonnet) to hunt Vane down. Rhett found Bonnet instead, and Vane escaped back to Nassau. From there he sailed on to meet up with Edward Teach at Ocracoke Inlet, perhaps intending to join forces with him, and the crews apparently spent a number of days getting gloriously drunk.

Later on in 1718 Vane, in charge of a brigantine and a small sloop, encountered a French warship which was mistaken for a rather more harmless merchantman. Realising his mistake and appreciating that he was out-gunned, Vane ordered the retreat. This led to accusations of cowardice being made against him and in the resulting democratic vote he was stripped of command by Rackham. Vane left with fifteen of his crew on board the sloop, carried on plundering shipping in the vicinity of the Bay Islands, but in February 1719 was hit by a hurricane which caused devastating damage. His sloop sank, and all but one of his crew were drowned, leaving Vane and the other survivor to fend for themselves on an uninhabited island.

For several months they survived on a diet of fish and turtles. Vane's ordeal was not over when an English ship under the command of Captain Holford called in to replenish water supplies. Holford was a former pirate who had accepted the King's Pardon and who recognised Vane from old. According to Johnson, he declined to offer safe passage to Vane, saying: 'Charles, I shan't trust you aboard my ship unless I carry you a prisoner; for I shall have you caballing with my men, knock me on the head, and run away with my ship a-pirating'.

Vane had to wait until another ship called in, but this time was successful in blagging his way aboard. According to Johnson, all went well until the captain of the new ship met up with Holford and invited him to share dinner. Holford saw Vane, revealed his identity to his dinner companion, and Vane was promptly arrested and taken to Jamaica in chains.

Normally the cycle of imprisonment, trial, sentence and execution was accomplished in a matter of weeks, if not days, but for some reason which is not clear, in Vane's case the period stretched to well over a year. He was finally tried on 22 March 1721, was found guilty, and was hanged off Port Royal's Gallows Point exactly one week later. From there his corpse was taken to Gun Cay, and left hanging in chains as a deterrent to others.

Setting aside the embellishments added by Johnson, what comes across is that Vane was a fine sailor with a cunning mind and loads of chutzpah. What also comes across is a man who alienated many because of his divisive behaviour, and whose cruelty and temper inspired fear but never engendered loyalty.

Stede Bonnet

Known on occasions as 'the Gentleman Pirate', and sometimes going by the name of Captain Thomas, Stede Bonnet was something of an oddity. In general, pirates consisted of men with a seafaring background – Bonnet had no maritime experience whatsoever. Most pirates started off by stealing or over-running the ship they were sailing aboard – Bonnet apparently went out and bought a vessel before equipping it for piracy. Most pirates dispensed with powdered wigs and tailored clothing – Bonnet insisted on retaining these vestiges of respectability.

According to *A General History*, he took up piracy due to a desire to escape his nagging wife. As Johnson put it: 'this Humour of going a-pyrating proceeded from a Disorder in his Mind … and which is said to have been occasioned by some Discomforts he found in a married State.' It sounds a slightly simplistic explanation as to why a man, born and brought up in comparative luxury on the island of Barbados, should walk out on his wife, three sons and a daughter at the age of 29. On paper, he was already wealthy, owning some 400 acres of land near Bridgetown, and had served in the island's militia with the rank of major. He may well have suffered a mental breakdown, possibly linked to the death of one of his sons, and there is also a suggestion that he had borrowed money, possibly after crops on his plantation had failed or been ruined by hurricanes. Certainly, his life as a pirate seems to have been engineered as an escape – although what he was running away from is not entirely clear.

He could afford to commission a local boat-builder to construct a sixty-ton sloop for him, armed with ten guns, which he christened *Revenge*. Rather to everyone's surprise he then recruited seventy seamen to crew his vessel – at a regular wage. This was unheard of, since pirates received no wage, merely sharing in any prizes captured during the voyage. His cover story was that he was intending to become an island trader, and in early summer 1717 he weighed anchor and started plundering off the coast of Virginia. In the case of Barbadian ships which he captured, such as the *Turbet*, he burned them afterwards, presumably to prevent news getting back to his friends and family on the island. The cargoes which he seized he then sold at Gardiners Island off New York, before heading down to the Carolinas. From there he sailed towards Nassau in the Bahamas. During the journey the *Revenge* was chased down by a Spanish man-of-war and in the ensuing firefight Bonnet was badly injured. Many of his crew were killed and the *Revenge* suffered serious damage.

It was obvious that Bonnet was no sailor, and the fractious crew were unhappy to continue under his leadership. At Nassau, Bonnet met up with Teach, and presumably to enable him to recover from his injuries, Bonnet ceded control of his ship to the more experienced Teach. He stayed on board, no doubt 'learning the ropes' and during the autumn of 1717 Teach and Bonnet sailed together on the *Revenge* as they successfully raided shipping in the vicinity of Delaware, capturing eleven vessels. The pair then split up for a while, with Teach sailing off in a newly captured ship *Concorde*, which he renamed *Queen Anne's Revenge*. Bonnet headed for the Western Caribbean but failed to capture the 400-ton merchantman *Protestant Caesar*. This was the final straw for the disgruntled crew and when Teach met up again with Bonnet, he relieved him of his command. Lieutenant Richards was put in charge of the *Revenge*, and Bonnet remained as 'house guest' on board *Queen Anne's Revenge*.

These two ships then sailed up to Charles Town and blockaded the town. By then news of the King's Pardon was known, and both Teach and Bonnet decided to take advantage of it, travelling overland to North Carolina's state capital of Bath in order to receive the pardon from Governor Charles Eden. By then, war between Britain and Spain had broken out again, and Bonnet received permission from Eden to head for the Danish island of St Thomas in the Virgin Isles, in the hope of obtaining a Letter of Marque. In early 1718 he retraced his footsteps to the *Revenge*, only to find Teach had got there first, had looted the *Revenge*, and taken all of its cargo and many of its supplies. Bonnet had to defer sailing for St Thomas, because the hurricane season had arrived. He was anxious not to let the Pardon lapse, but at the same time he needed to obtain fresh supplies, and that meant more piracy. He picked up eleven men who had been marooned and left to die by Teach, changed the name of the *Revenge* to *Royal James*, and started styling himself 'Captain Thomas'. The name chosen for the ship makes it fairly clear that Bonnet had Jacobite sympathies and was not a fan of the House of Hanover, which had taken over the monarchy in Britain some four years earlier.

The *Royal James* headed for Delaware. By then (August 1718) it was clear that the ship was in need of careening and repair. On his way to Delaware Bay Bonnet seized upwards of ten small ships, using the timber from some of them to effect the repairs which were carried out at the mouth of the Cape Fear River, at what is now called Bonnet Point. This part of the Cape Fear River was technically under the jurisdiction of North Carolina, but Governor Johnson of South Carolina (who had suffered the ignominy of being blockaded by Teach and Bonnet at Charles Town) was determined to exact revenge.

Governor Johnson commissioned Colonel William Rhett to take a naval force of two ships, the *Sea Nymph* and the *Henry*, each with eight guns, and to capture the *Royal James*. On the evening of 26 September the two sloops entered the mouth of the river and were spotted by Bonnet, who hastily brought all his crew on board his flagship. The following morning he tried to escape the trap set for him by Rhett but the low water meant that ships from both sides ran aground and were trapped until high tide. For five frustrating hours the beached ships exchanged musket fire as the crews waited for the tide to free them. In the event *Sea Nymph* and *Henry* were the first to float free, while the *Royal James* was still stuck fast. This enabled Rhett in his two sloops to close in on the stranded vessel. Bonnet had no choice but to surrender: the *Royal James* was captured and Bonnet and his surviving crew were hauled off for trial in Charles Town.

For three weeks Bonnet was held under house arrest, in the home of the Provost Marshall, separated from most of the rest of his crew. On 24 October he managed to escape, probably with the help of a local trader, and hid up on Sullivan's Island. The indefatigable Colonel Rhett was put in charge of a posse which searched the island and eventually succeeded in recapturing Bonnet, after shooting dead one of his co-escapees.

By the time Bonnet was brought before Sir Nicholas Trott for trial on 10 November many of his crew had already been sentenced to death. After delivering a lengthy peroration based on Christian doctrines, Trott announced the death penalty on Bonnet, who had conducted his own defence after being denied Counsel. He had also been denied the chance to bring forward witnesses to the effect that his crew had forced him to break the terms of his original Pardon. Bonnet pleaded for clemency, and sentence was deferred on seven occasions, before Bonnet was led to the gallows on 10 December. In all, thirty-five pirates were hanged. Two men who had given evidence against Bonnet were pardoned and four men were acquitted.

The trial reports have proved to be an invaluable resource in detailing the events leading up to Bonnet's death, and suggest that Bonnet was either of such a weak mental state, or was so dominated by his crew (in particular the quartermaster) that he was really not responsible for the actions carried out in his name. Nowadays he would have been declared as being of unsound mind, but in the eighteenth century, before a court presided over by the pirate-hating Sir Nicholas Trott, there was no question of any such leniency.

William Fly

Captain Fly deserves a mention precisely because his career was so short and unspectacular; his demise after a career lasting only a matter of weeks shows how quickly the net closed in on piracy at the end of the so-called Golden Age. From then on, pirates knew that they were simply not going to get away with it.

Nothing is known of the origins of William Fly. He may well have been born in England, and is rumoured to have earned a living as a bare-knuckle prize fighter. He was reputed to be a man with a violent temper and a short fuse. Another rumour bases him in Jamaica, and certainly that is where he was picked up as bosun by Captain John Green on board the ship *Elizabeth*, on a journey to the coast of West Africa. To have been bosun, he must have been an experienced seaman. The voyage started in April 1726. One month later, at one in the morning, Fly led an insurrection which resulted in the captain being dragged from his cabin and forced overboard. In desperation the captain caught hold of the main sail, and had to be physically made to let go when an axe was brought down on his hand. He was left to drown. Moments later, the first mate Thomas Jenkins suffered the same fate – he too was attacked with the axe before toppling overboard and drowning. The mutineers then elected Fly as their captain. The ship's name was changed to *Fame's Revenge*, and off she sailed to the coast of North Carolina. In the space of two months they captured five sloops, none of them with a particularly remunerative cargo. One of the men captured by Fly was an experienced mariner from the port of Bristol called Captain Atkinson, and he was forced to join the pirates as they headed up the coast towards New England. At one point, half the pirates gave chase to another vessel, leaving Fly and a few men on board *Fame's Revenge* with Atkinson. Seizing his moment, Atkinson turned the tables on Fly and his fellow-pirates, put them in irons, and took them off to be tried at the Admiralty Court. Justice was swift, and on 12 July 1726 William Fly was publicly hanged in Boston harbour.

The trial report, with the somewhat unwieldy title of: 'The Tryals of sixteen persons for piracy, &c. Four of which were found guilty, and the rest acquitted. At a special Court of Admiralty for the Tryal of Pirates, held at Boston within the province of the Masachusetts-Bay in New-England, on Monday the fourth day of July, anno dom. 1726', can still be accessed via the Evans Early American Imprint Collection.

What gave Fly a measure of notoriety was that he refused to admit his crimes, or to show any remorse whatsoever. This was despite the fact that the authorities allowed Cotton Mather, a reverend gentleman of considerable renown, to try and intercede with Fly to get him to repent. Far from it. Fly despised the church almost as much as he hated any form of authority. It is said that on the day of his execution he leaped aboard the cart taking him to the site of the gallows (thereby avoiding the humiliation of being put in chains). He mounted the step, nosegay in hand, and then tore a strip off the hangman for making a slip-shod job of tying the noose correctly. It is said that he used his rope skills to retie the knot properly, put his neck in the noose, and defiantly addressed the crowd with a tirade against the injustice of sea-captains. Johnson reported, in the second edition of *A General History of the Pyrates*, that Fly demanded that 'all Masters of Vessels might take Warning of the Fate of the Captain that he had murder'd, and to pay Sailors their Wages when due'.

A hanging scene – in this case with Stede Bonnet being hanged.

After Fly was hanged, the same fate was doled out to his fellow mutineers and in Fly's case his body was gibbeted on Nixes Mate Island, in Boston harbour, as a warning to others not to try to follow his example. Johnson ended his chapter with the words:

> *Thus ended the short Reign of an obdurate Wretch, who only wanted Skill and Power to be as infamous as any who had scoured the Seas; the Names of the three pyrates, executed with him, were Samuel Cole, George Condick and Henry Greenvill.*

Olivier Levasseur

It would be a mistake to assume that pirates all came from the British Isles – in fact they were a cosmopolitan lot. A look at the list of nationalities of crew members aboard captured pirate ships show sailors from many northern European counties, as well as a significant number of sailors who had been former slaves. In the case of Olivier Levasseur he was born in France, served in the French navy, fought against the British, but ended up sailing on board the *Postillion* alongside a number of British pirates including Hornigold (from 1716) and Bellamy (from 1717).

His nickname was *La Buse* – the Buzzard – on account of the speed and ruthlessness with which he launched attacks. He may also have been more properly known as Louis Labous, or as Olivier Vasseur or Oliver La Bouche. He was probably thirty years old when, in 1720, he joined forces with Howell Davis and Thomas Cocklyn to raid the West African slave port of Ouidah, in modern-day Benin, reducing the town to rubble. From there he sailed round the Cape and up the eastern coast of Africa before becoming shipwrecked on one of the Comoros islands.

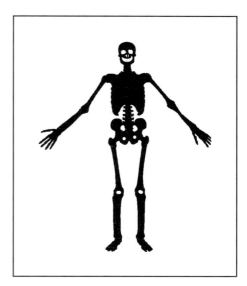

The flag of Olivier Levasseur.

By the time he was rescued he had become blind in one eye (a legacy of a sword injury incurred early in his career) but whether or not he wore an eye-patch, giving rise to the typical image of a pirate, is not recorded at the time and may well have been a subsequent embellishment to the story. He moved his centre of operations to Sainte-Marie, a small island off the north-eastern coast of Madagascar. Here, jointly with a number of other pirates such as Edward England, he could harass shipping using the trade routes favoured by the various East India companies, as well as lying in wait for the annual treasure fleet belonging to the Great Mughal.

With his ship *Le Victorieux* he went into partnership with an English pirate called John Taylor, in charge of the *Defence*, and together they captured a rich merchant ship named after the Laccadives, a group of tiny islands off the coast of India, seizing merchandise worth £75,000. They then patrolled the area of the Indian Ocean around Réunion and in time stumbled across one of the wealthiest cargoes ever taken by pirates.

Violent storms in the area had hit a Portuguese galleon carrying a vast amount of treasure from the Portuguese colony of Goa, back to Portugal. On board were several notable individuals including Dom Sebastião de Andrade, who was the Bishop of Goa (known as the Patriarch of the East Indies). Another was Dom Luís Carlos Inácio Xavier de Meneses, fifth Count of Ericeira, the Portuguese Viceroy of Goa. Their ship, variously known as *Nossa Senhora do Cabo (Our Lady of the Cape)* or *Virgem Do Cabo (The Virgin of the Cape)*, had originally been carrying seventy-four guns (thirty six on each side, plus two positioned aft). When the storm struck these were jettisoned. A 'loose cannon' could easily wreck a ship's timbers, even one the size of the galleon, and clearing the decks of the guns would have made the ship considerably lighter and more manoeuvrable. Unfortunately, it also meant that she was utterly defenceless when the storm abated and she called in at Réunion to effect repairs.

Levasseur and his co-conspirators would not have believed their good fortune when they were able to capture the vessel without a significant fight. The hoard of gold on board which was seized was staggering: each pirate is reported to have received 50,000 guineas as well as forty-two diamonds and other precious stones. There were pearls, there were rich silks and there were treasure chests of silver. Indeed, there was so much treasure that one story says that the pirates did not even bother to rob the captives of personal items, or hold them to ransom.

One problem is that 50,000 guineas per pirate is unrealistic given that there were believed to be over 700 crew members spread between three, or possibly four ships. There was Levasseur, there was John Taylor, there was Edward England and, possibly, a pirate called Jaspar Seagar. The latter may, or may not, have been the same Seager as the pirate more usually known by the name of Edward England.

More realistic would have been a hoard of gold which was divided between the three or four ships, giving a share of 50,000 guineas per vessel. Even that begs the question: why guineas? These were, after all, minted in Britain for use in Britain, not as a worldwide currency. Far more likely, given the port of origin, was that the ship was carrying either Portuguese moidores or Indian rupiya. It was only in 1717 that the East India Company obtained permission to open a Mint in Bombay, producing gold coins called carolinas. Certainly, guineas were unlikely to have been available in Goa in any significant quantities.

The Bishop was apparently escorting home a treasure known as the Flaming Cross of Goa – a 2 metre high solid-gold cross studded with emeralds, diamonds and rubies. It was reported to be so heavy that it needed three men just to lift it and transport it onto Levasseur's ship.

There are, however, problems with this mythical cross: it was never mentioned at any stage prior to its fateful voyage. One would have expected someone to have noticed it in the cathedral at Goa, or realised that it was being lugged away to a waiting galleon. And why would a cross of solid gold be 2 metres tall, when that would suggest that it would weigh a massive four tons, far more than could be carried by three men? It sounds more probable that any such cross was made of wood inlaid with stones and precious metals. And if the usual hyperbole of eighteenth-century pirate storytellers is stripped away, was the cross really 2 metres tall – or merely a cross held aloft by a procession following behind the Bishop as he went about his perambulations? Any advance on 1 metre? Any advance on a bit of filigree gilding and a few precious stones?

Notwithstanding such cynicism, it has been estimated that the plunder seized from the stricken galleon would nowadays be worth in excess of a billion pounds, making Levasseur one of the wealthiest pirates in history. The size of the treasure seized from the Portuguese may have been somewhat exaggerated, but these stories went on to inspire Stevenson with his story of the capture of the *Viceroy of India* in his book *Treasure Island*. Lovers of film-lore will know that Basil Rathbone played the part of Levasseur in the 1935 Errol Flynn film entitled *Captain Blood*.

What happened to Levasseur is not clear. He is assumed to have returned to Sainte-Marie, still in partnership with Taylor. By then Levasseur had renamed the captured galleon *Victorieux*, and together they captured two vessels belonging to the French East India Company, *La Duchesse de Noailles* and *La Ville d'Ostende*. Taylor and Levasseur then appear to have had differences of opinion and they went their separate ways – Taylor back to the Caribbean, Levasseur back to Madagascar. Levasseur is then thought to have retired from piracy and is rumoured to have settled on one of the islands in the Seychelles. Years passed, until he apparently wanted to take advantage of a general pardon on offer from the French king, but his overtures to the local governor on Réunion was rebuffed; he could only get the pardon if he surrendered much of the treasure. Levasseur declined.

One story has it that Levasseur got bored (presumably from admiring his gold cross and from re-counting his guineas) and wanted to use his knowledge of the coastline around Madagascar by continuing to act as a pilot, assisting local shipping. It sounds slightly improbable given his staggering wealth. But on one such piloting exercise off Fort Dauphin on the coast of Madagascar he was apparently recognised, taken to Réunion, and imprisoned at Saint-Paul. Another version of this states that he was captured by a Captain L'Hermitte who had been sent by Governor Dumas specifically to search for Levasseur. He was brought to Réunion on board *La Meduse*, interrogated by the authorities and on 3 July was condemned to death. He was hanged for piracy four days later. Just before the execution he is supposed to have taken off the necklace which he was wearing, and which reputedly contained a cryptogram identifying where his treasure could be found, hurling it into the crowd with the words "Mes trésors à qui saura comprendre!' ('My treasures go to the one who can understand it!').

It all sounds like good theatre – after all, the condemned man would surely have had his hands tied, and is hardly likely to have been in a position to hurl a necklace into the crowd. There are so many inconsistencies, but they have never been allowed to get in the way of a story of lost treasure, of strange pictures carved on rocks, of pirate corpses with gold earrings found guarding hidden caves and of attempts to locate the missing treasure. These tales have perhaps more to do with boosting tourism in any number of supposed locations for the treasure – Réunion, Sainte-Marie, Madagascar, as well as on Mahé and Frégate Island in the Seychelles – than they have with any genuine treasure hunt.

Similarly, no one knows what happened to the cryptogram hurled into the crowd – and yet a copy mysteriously appeared some years later, incorporating all manner of hidden clues, strange alphabets, references to the Labours of Hercules, the Clavicles of Solomon, the signs of the zodiac and other matters more appropriate to a Dan Brown novel.

This myth of buried treasure is followed up in chapter 14. Fact and fiction are difficult to separate. For instance, the graveyard at Saint-Paul on the island of Réunion contains what is supposed to be the grave of La Buse. Given that the cemetery did not open until 1788, well over half a century after Levasseur's death, it is highly implausible. Besides, suicide victims and hanged criminals were not buried in cemeteries, and the records suggest that Levasseur's corpse was simply tossed into a communal grave immediately after the hanging. That has not prevented the gravestone becoming a shrine, visited by thousands of tourists, no

A copy of the cryptogram allegedly thrown to the crowd by Levasseur as he was led to the gallows.

doubt hoping for some miraculous sign leading them to the hiding place of his fabulous treasures.

Of course, every word written about *La Buse* may have been true. It is also possible that, without the testimony of self-interested raconteurs, posterity might never have known about the size of the treasure, or of the cryptogram – or even of the execution itself. Independent contemporary verification is sadly lacking.

Chapter 11

John Rackham, with Biographies of Anne Bonny and Mary Read

'Calico Jack' Rackham

It is difficult to escape the conclusion that Captain John Rackham (otherwise Rackam, but more generally known as 'Calico Jack' on account of his penchant for wearing clothing made of unbleached cotton) was no different to many other rank–and–file

A woodcut of Calico Jack Rackham.

pirates. He is famous for two things – for popularising the skull and crossed swords as his pirate flag, and, more significantly, for his association with not one but two female pirates. They were Anne Bonny and Mary Read. Ever since they were mentioned in Johnson's *A General History* these two women have captured the imagination, but take them out of Calico Jack's story and his life was somewhat mundane.

He is believed to have been born in England on Boxing Day 1682, and the circumstances in which he crossed the Atlantic and became a sailor are unrecorded. His career in piracy did not really get under way until 1718 when he was appointed quartermaster to Captain Vane on board the *Ranger*.

Later, and as already mentioned in the story of Charles Vane, the pair decided to go their separate ways after Rackham had led a group of malcontents who objected to Vane's captaincy. Only fifteen of the ninety-strong crew supported Vane, who was given control of a smaller ship and sent off with his loyal crew, and a small supply of stores and ammunition.

Rackham went off to raid shipping off Cuba, the Bahamas and up to Bermuda. In the course of these raids he seized the wealthy merchant ship *Kingston*, and made her his flagship. Unfortunately for Rackham, the seizure was observed onshore by Jamaican merchants and they immediately clamoured for pirate hunters to set off in hot pursuit as the *Kingston* headed off towards Cuba. By the time the pursuers caught up, Rackham had stopped by the Cuban island of Isla de los Pinos. He hid in the woods with most of his crew until the pursuers gave up their search for him.

The pursuers did, however, seize the *Kingston* and sailed off in her, along with her valuable cargo which Rackham had not had time to sell and distribute. Rackham was forced to go off and attempt to seize an English sloop, which had been captured by the Spanish. He succeeded in taking her from right under the noses of a Spanish warship, which was helpless to pursue them in the shallow waters off Cuba.

When the King's Pardon became known, and fearing that he was likely to be caught either by the bounty hunters out of Jamaica or the Spanish warships out of Cuba, Rackham decided things were getting too hot for him. He surrendered to Woodes Rogers, the new Governor of the Bahamas, at New Providence Island. He applied to be pardoned and this was granted in May 1719.

Spending his time in the bars of New Providence, Rackham fell for the easy charms of Anne Bonny, then married to another sailor by the name of John Bonny. John was in the employ of Woodes Rogers, the new governor, and had demanded that his wife should be flogged for her adulterous behaviour. The Rackham/Bonny relationship scandalised local society and the pair had to escape the island in 1719 on board a stolen sloop.

The next couple of months were spent looting and being a pain in the neck to fishermen and owners of small merchant ships in the Caribbean. A schooner and seven fishing boats were seized – but, it has to be said, these were little more than open canoes and the haul would have been of little commercial value. At one stage they seized the small but very fast sloop the *William*. She had four guns and was intended to have a crew of just fourteen. Rackham used this as his flagship. Eventually, just off the tip of Western Jamaica, the *William* was cornered by a Royal Navy vessel called the *Tyger* (also described as being the *Snow Tyger*) commanded by pirate hunter Jonathan Barnet. He had heard of a proclamation issued by Woodes Rogers in September 1720 declaring the earlier pardon void, and offering a reward for Rackham's capture. Barnet had on board a group of British soldiers, in addition to around twenty royal Navy sailors. The *Tyger* was well armed and encountered Rackham and his crew while they were at Dry Harbour Bay. Here they had spent the previous night getting thoroughly drunk after an encounter with another group of nine pirates. The *William* was at anchor when the *Tyger* approached them at night. The men on board the *William* were in no position to put up any resistance, having been drinking for many hours, and although there was a belated attempt to raise the anchor and set the sails, the *William* suffered serious damage and those on board were soon captured. Allegedly there were only two people on board who offered any serious resistance, both of them women. One was Anne Bonny and the other was Mary Read, both of them mentioned in more detail shortly.

Rackham was taken prisoner and escorted to Jamaica's capital, where he was tried for piracy along with nine of his men. All were executed on 17/18 November 1720. Five, including Rackham, were hanged from the gallows which had been erected at Gallows Point at Port Royal, between the high and low tide marks. The others met their fate the next day at Kingston. Later, Rackham's body was cut down, gibbetted, and left hanging at the entrance of the main harbour near what is now known as Rackham's Cay 'as an example to others'. In a separate trial, the nine pirates with whom Rackham had been carousing before his arrest were also tried. Records show that six were hanged, with no record as to the fate of the other three.

So, we are left with a man who was a pirate for barely two years, who mostly captured fishing vessels and ships with low-value cargoes, who was never particularly brave or ferocious, and who was happy to accept a pardon and then go back on his word after he fell for the charms of Anne Bonny. Of such meagre exploits are stories of swashbuckling heroics readily made. He was 37 when he died.

Anne Bonny

Ever since the exploits of Anne Bonny and Mary Read were mentioned by Johnson in his *A General History*, the pair have captured the public imagination. Originally it may have been horror at the idea of women behaving as bravely and violently as men. Maybe they appealed to repressed women everywhere, who saw them as 'freedom fighters' just as modern readers may see them as figureheads in a move towards equality. Their story has been embroidered to fit the message, and it is difficult to unravel the threads to see exactly where the truth lies.

One thing is clear: they were little more than an addendum to the history of piracy. They captained no ships, they captured no significant treasure, they did no more than fight alongside the criminal element that they befriended – and when the chips were down they 'pleaded their bellies' (i.e., claimed that they were pregnant) in order to avoid the hangman's noose. Their menfolk on the other hand went to the gallows. It is also worth remembering that for all the tales of derring-do, their career as pirates spanned exactly two months – from 22 August to 22 October 1720.

Anne Bonny was in all probability born near Cork in Ireland in 1698. She appears to have been the illegitimate daughter of William Cormac, an Irish lawyer, after he had an affair with his housemaid called Mary Brennan. William and his wife separated following the discovery of the affair, and William was left to bring up the child. His legal practice evaporated as the public recoiled against the idea of him cohabiting with his mistress, and the trio left for Charles Town (now Charleston) in South Carolina to make a new life for themselves.

Anne's mother Mary contracted typhoid, leaving the 13-year-old Anne to face a difficult period in her life largely unsupervised, but required to run her father's household. Numerous stories concern her teenage years – that she stabbed another girl to death with a table knife, and another that she was sexually assaulted by a man who she subsequently beat up so badly that he was hospitalised. As Johnson described it: '...once, when a young Fellow would have lain with her, against her Will, she beat him so, that he lay ill of it a considerable Time.'

Her father sought to marry her off, but the chosen groom did not appeal to Anne. Instead, at the age of 16 she fell for the charms of a petty criminal and sailor called James Bonny. He whisked her off to the Bahamas, where he seems to have obtained a job passing information to Governor Rogers about the activities of various pirates operating from the islands. Anne grew tired of living with a snitch – her drinking friends in the taverns were pirates with whom she shared her favours. As Johnson wrote, she was 'not altogether so reserved in point of Chastity', and stated that James Bonny once 'surprised her lying in a hammock with another man'. There has to be a strong inference that Anne resorted to prostitution, possibly with the full knowledge of her husband.

As already described, she then deserted her husband and ran off with Jack Rackham. There are stories that she became pregnant and went to Cuba in order to give birth to her chid, but what happened to the infant is not recorded. There are also stories that she disguised herself as a man while on board with Rackham, but this all sounds somewhat far-fetched. In the confines of a small ship even the least observant crew member would surely have picked up on the fact that the captain was having an affair with one of the crew, however much (s)he disguised herself with men's clothing. At her subsequent trial, one of the witnesses is reported to have stated that Anne only dressed as a man when going into combat, and that she dressed as a woman the rest of the time. Dorothy Thomas, a woman who claimed to have been captured and placed on board Rackham's ship, gave testimony to the fact that Bonny and Read were known by everyone to be female 'by the largeness of their breasts'.

Another captive said of Read and Bonny that they 'were both very profligate, cursing and swearing much, and very ready and willing to do anything on board'. Johnson describes Anne as a brave fighter and states that although she and Mary Read put up stiff resistance when their ship was overrun by men under the command of Jonathan Barnet on the *Tyger*, their example was not followed by any of the men on board the *William*.

They were captured and their trial on Jamaica was held separately from that of Rackham and the rest of his crew. Anne claimed that she was 'quick with child' – an expression describing the stage in pregnancy where the movement of the foetus can be detected (typically at around seventeen to eighteen weeks). The law prohibited the taking of the life of an unborn child and therefore Anne, found guilty and sentenced to hang, had her sentence suspended. The story told by Johnson is that Anne was allowed one last chance to see Rackham before he was led to the gallows – and is supposed to have admonished him with the words: 'Had you fought like a man, you need not have been hang'd like a dog.' It sounds good, but whether the authorities really allowed such a meeting, or whether she uttered those stirring words, is far from clear.

There are numerous stories as to what happened next, with some suggesting that Anne's father re-entered the scene, paid a large sum of money to get his daughter out of jail, and that she went off and married a man called Jospeh Burleigh, settled in South Carolina, had eight children, and died on 25 April 1782. By then she would have been in her mid-eighties and was reportedly buried somewhere in York County Virginia.

Another story has Anne released from prison and disappearing into the stews of the Jamaican underworld, or of her changing her identity and resuming the life of a pirate. The fact remains: there are no accurate records, but interestingly Johnson heavily embellished his tale of Anne Bonny in his second edition of *A General History*. By then he would have realised the potential for stirring up public interest in this 'remarkable' woman, and he milked the story for all it was worth. Suffice to say, the public wanted her to be a heroic figure, they wanted to believe that a woman could succeed in a man's world, they wanted to believe that she could 'get away with it'.

Later embellishments include the suggestion that Anne and Mary were lovers, that Anne settled in the South of England and ended her days running a tavern before spending a genteel retirement tending her roses. Another happy-ever-after tale has Anne and Mary escaping from prison, moving to Louisiana together, setting up home and bringing up their children as one big happy family.

The one truth remains: the only thing which distinguished Anne Bonny from all the other anonymous crew members of pirate ships was her gender. She was not particularly successful, she was not a role model who inspired others of her generation to take up piracy – she was a petty criminal who just happened to be a woman. However, the passing centuries have elevated her to a status she never earned or deserved, and it is fair to say that she has inspired more stories in books and in films than almost any other pirate. Most recently the character of Angelica, played by Penelope Cruz in the 2011 film *Pirates of the Caribbean: on Stranger Tides* owes much to the story of Anne Bonny. In recent years various plays have explored a lesbian relationship between the two women. Perhaps that tells us rather more about the preoccupations of our current world than it ever does about what really happened 300 years ago.

Mary Read

Mary Read was probably born in Devon, some time between 1685 and 1690, the illegitimate daughter of a recently widowed woman. Her mother had previously been married to a sea captain, by whom she had a legitimate (male) child. Mother supposedly sought to hide her daughter's existence from the parents of her late husband – she feared the loss of the financial support she received from them. When the boy died, mother was left with a quandary, but one which was quickly resolved by passing the young girl off as her deceased half-brother. Mary was therefore brought up in boy's clothing, was known as Mark, and in her teenage years became a footman to a wealthy Frenchwoman living in London. Bored with this, she decided to go to sea.

Later, she jumped ship and enlisted in a British Regiment of Foot, and served in Flanders. In a subsequent change of direction she enlisted in a cavalry regiment, where she met and fell in love with a fellow soldier. She revealed her gender, married her man, and set up as tavern-keeper at The Three Horseshoes ('De drie hoefijzers') at Breda Castle in Holland. When her husband died a few months later, Mary tried to re-enlist in the army but failed to settle and headed for the Caribbean aboard a Dutch ship, disguised as a man.

At this point in the story Mary was treading a path already established by a surprising number of other women. The eighteenth century has many examples of cross-dressers – of men who adopted a female persona (such as the eccentric and flamboyant Chevalier d'Eon) and of women enlisting in the army to serve alongside boyfriends and siblings. It appears that this was sometimes accepted (tacitly at least) by the authorities, as in the case of Phoebe Hessel, who was born in 1718 and died at the age of 108. Her gravestone in Brighton records:

> *She served for many years, as a private soldier in the 5th Regiment of Foot, in different parts of Europe, and in the year 1745 fought under the command of the Duke of Cumberland at the Battle of Fontenoy, where she received a bayonet wound in the arm.*

Phoebe served in the army for over seventeen years, and did so in order to be close to her boyfriend, who served in the same regiment. Following her injury she was discharged from the army, eventually receiving a pension of 10*s* 6*d* a week. By then her gender was known to officers in the regiment, not least because on one occasion she was ordered to be stripped to the waist so that a public lashing could be administered. Her story made her famous and she was given the nickname of 'the Amazon of Stepney'.

Plays and books in the eighteenth century were full of tales about lovelorn young girls enlisting in foreign wars in order not to be separated from the object of their love. Coincidentally, many of the women came from Holland – at least ten were 'uncovered' in the 1720s. Even in the Royal Navy female sailors were not unknown, despite the fact that Admiralty Regulations stated that women were not allowed to be taken to sea and that '… no women be ever permitted to be on board but such as are really the wives of the men they come to, and the ship not too much pestered even with them'. When Admiral Cuthbert Collingwood, a contemporary of Nelson, discovered that women had been brought on board his flagship, he ordered the women ashore pointing out that 'I never knew a woman brought to sea in a ship that some mischief did not befall the vessel'. But women did go aboard ships, and one particular female who captured the public imagination was Hannah Snell. She served for three years in the Navy before revealing her gender to her shipmates. After being injured eleven times in her legs, she petitioned the Duke of Cumberland for a pension. She sold her story to the publisher Robert Walker and the book appeared in print as *The Female Soldier*, running to two editions. Hannah also appeared on stage in army uniform presenting military drills and singing songs, firmly establishing the heroic image of the female soldier.

But Mary Read went one stage further when she became a pirate. It is suggested that the ship which she was on was captured by Captain Rackham, and that she bravely resisted capture, earning the respect of Rackham – so much so that s(he) was offered quarter if s(he) joined their merry band. By this time the crew included Anne Bonny, and the story goes that Anne recognised Mary's gender and befriended her to the extent that Rackham became jealous of Anne's relationship with someone who appeared to be 'another man'. Anne therefore had to spill the beans and Rackham sailed on his way knowing that two women were serving on board. Other, more embroidered, versions refer to the lesbian activities of the two women, while others allude to a *ménage à trois*.

The story continues that Mary fell in love with one of the other sailors, but that the object of her love had offended an older more experienced sailor, who challenged the young man to a duel. Fearing that her lover would be killed in the duel, Mary took it upon herself to take his place in the fight. She won, and killed the old pirate. The tale is embellished by stories that halfway through the fight she distracted her opponent by whipping off her top and baring her breasts; the poor bloke was so put out to find that he was fighting a woman that before he knew it Mary had seized her cutlass, cut off his arm, and severed his head. Later, when the *William* was attacked by pirate-hunter Jonathan Barnet, she allegedly fought on deck as a number of male sailors fled below deck; she demanded that they come back up and fight, yelling 'If there's a man among ye, ye'll come up and fight like the man ye are to be!' No one responded, so she fired a shot into the hold, killing one pirate and wounding another.

Whether this story of bravery and courage actually happened is open to doubt, but it suited Johnson to spread the story. What is known is that Mary was sent for trial and, like Anne Bonny, was found guilty of piracy. She apparently listened to the judge as he solemnly announced:

> *You Mary Read and Anne Bonney, alias Bon, are to go from hence to the place from whence you came, and from thence to the place of execution; where you shall be severally hanged by the neck till you are severally dead. And God of his infinite Mercy be merciful to both your souls.*

Then, and only then, did she inform the court that she was 'quick with child'. She was therefore imprisoned pending the conclusion of her pregnancy. She supposedly addressed the court about her fate, saying that, 'as to hanging, it is no great hardship. For were it not for that, every cowardly fellow would turn pirate and so unfit the sea, that men of courage must starve.'

Once in prison it appears that she caught a violent fever and died a few months later, in all likelihood while still pregnant. Records show that she was buried on 28 April 1721 at St Catherine's church in Jamaica.

Cutting aside the flannel and hyperbole which was Johnson's hallmark, we are left with a female forced from an early age to masquerade as a man, living a life which was not at any stage easy. She may well have been brave and courageous, but she was dead by her mid-thirties. Her story quickly inspired authors and playwrights, one of the earliest being John Gay. As a follow-up to *Beggar's Opera* in 1729 he wrote *Polly*, the story of Polly Peachum who travels to the New World and takes up piracy while she searches for her husband Macheath. Although the Lord Chancellor banned the performance of the opera as being libelous and highly critical of the government of the day, the ban only served to fuel *Polly*'s popularity and Gay made many thousands of pounds out of sales of the written version – even though it was not performed on stage until 1777.

It is quite possible that Johnson invented the idea of crossdressing for the second edition of *A General History*. In doing so he tapped into a rich vein of interest in the whole idea of a woman taking on the persona of a man. Throughout the eighteenth century the public flocked to see plays in which women dressed as men – known as breeches parts, although this may not necessarily have been because the play explored female sexuality and power; more a case of being able to leer at a woman wearing trousers and showing far more leg than was normal. The Georgians loved to be shocked by gender transpositions, and if nothing else, *A General History* shows that stories of scandalous behaviour were good for book sales.

Anne Bonny.

The idea of a female buccaneer has remained a popular concept, as evidenced by the film *Cutthroat Island* made in 1995 – at a cost of $98 million. It recovered a mere $10 million at the Box Office, and probably did more than any other film to put Hollywood off making pirate blockbusters until *Pirates of the Caribbean* came along. In *Cutthroat Island*, Geena Davis plays the part of a pirate's daughter involved in a race against her rivals to find a hidden island that contains a fabulous treasure. All the usual ingredients of hokum are there, but even giving it a female lead could not save it from being a turkey.

Right: Mary Read.

Below: An engraving of 'Anne Bonny and Mary Read'. It was used as a double-page pull-out in the 1725 edition of the *General History of the Pyrates*.

Ann Bonny *and* Mary Read *convicted of Piracy Nov.* 28*th* 1720 *a Court of Vice Admiralty held at* St Jago de la Vega *in ye Island of Jam*

Chapter 12

Killed in Action: Biographies of Edward Teach, Howell Davis and John ('Bartholomew') Roberts

Edward Teach – Blackbeard

Of all the pirates in the so-called 'Golden Age' none typified the image of the swashbuckling buccaneer better than the man still known as 'Blackbeard'. Much of what we know about his exploits comes from Johnson's *History of the Pyrates*, and the ten pages in that book which are devoted to Blackbeard help paint the picture of a man of 'uncommon Boldness and personal Courage'.

Johnson states that Edward Teach was born in Bristol, was in the Royal Navy during the War of Spanish Succession, and did not hold a command until 'he went a pyrating' towards the end of 1716. Johnson helps show him as a man of appalling depravity, mentioning his fourteen wives, the last of whom he married when she was sixteen. After he had lain with his wife all night, it was, says Johnson, Blackbeard's custom 'to invite five or six of his brutal Companions to come ashore, and he would force her to prostitute herself to them all, one after another, before his Face'. No wonder genteel English readers were fascinated, but horrified, by his wanton behaviour.

Johnson also pays much attention to Blackbeard's image – and in particular his beard – saying that it was 'like a frightful meteor, which covered his whole face', and that it frightened America more than any comet that had appeared there for a long time. 'The Beard was black, which he suffered to grow of an extravagant Length', and apparently he twisted the ends and tucked them in behind his ears. At times of battle, he was stated to have threaded slow burning fuses into his knotted beard; '… his eyes naturally looking fierce and wild, making him altogether such a Figure, that imagination cannot form an Idea of a Fury, from Hell, to look more frightful'. This perhaps was Blackbeard's secret: he looked the part. He did not have to behave with extreme cruelty, he just had to look ferocious, sword in hand, three brace of pistols 'hanging in Holsters like Bandoliers', and with oily smoke swirling around his dark face. No wonder that on many occasions his victims gave up without a fight.

His surname was variously given as Thatch, Thack, Theach and Titche; the wide range of monikers may have been an attempt to 'protect the good name of his family', or may simply reflect the fact that in an age of widespread illiteracy, spelling accurately was not especially important and even legal documents often used different spelling in the same official deed. He may well have been living in Jamaica when he started off as an apprentice to Hornigold. He moved his operations to the Bahamas and while working with Hornigold captured a French merchant ship called *La Concord*. At the time the vessel was just 100 miles off Martinique, on a mission to deliver slaves to that island. She was able to offer little resistance when Teach appeared on the scene, because the French crew had already suffered a number of casualties including thirty-six crewmen who were suffering from scurvy and dysentery. Teach, in command of two sloops, one with 120 men and a dozen cannon, the other with thirty men and eight cannon, quickly captured *La Concord* with the minimum of damage caused. The cabin boy on *La Concord* informed Teach where the captain had hidden a cache of gold dust – and was rewarded by being allowed to join Teach's crew. Three other crew volunteered to join Teach, and a further ten were forced to join – pilots, cooks, carpenters and surgeons. Teach was happy to allow the remaining captives, including the captain, to continue their journey on one of his own sloops – Teach had his eyes on converting *La Concorde* into a fighting machine the likes of which had not been seen in the Caribbean.

She was refurbished as a battleship, armed with forty cannon, and re-named the *Queen Anne's Revenge*. On his new flagship Teach caused mayhem as he sailed northward up the Lower Antilles, from Bequia to St Vincent, St Lucia, Nevis, and Antigua, seizing shipping along the way. By early December 1717 he had reached Puerto Rico. Four months later he was in the Bay of Honduras, and while there captured the sloop *Adventure*, under the captaincy of David Herriot. The reluctant captain was forced to join the pirates as they sailed in a small but powerful flotilla up past the Caymen Islands towards Cuba. Teach then settled on a really audacious plan – to sail up to the major South Carolina port of Charles Town and to blockade it, holding it to ransom. In particular he was in urgent need of medical supplies. The blockade lasted a week, during which time a number of vessels, including the *Crowley* were captured. Teach then threatened to kill all the prisoners taken on board the *Crowley* unless a medicine chest was delivered to him. The 'ransom' was brought to him, and the prisoners were released unharmed, leaving Teach to sail northwards towards Old Topsail Inlet (now known as Beaufort Inlet) in North Carolina.

What happened next is clear enough – both the *Queen Anne's Revenge* and the sloop *Adventure* ran aground. 'Why' is not so clear – the captured Captain David Herriot later stated that he thought that the grounding, on a sandbar across the front of the inlet, was deliberate. By then, Teach's followers numbered more than 300 men, and he may have been keen to retain the plunder himself, casting many of the crew ashore. Whatever the reason, Teach was able to sail away from the inlet with all of the spoils and a very much smaller, hand-picked, crew.

A few months later (June 1718), Teach and perhaps twenty of his crew reached Ocracoke Inlet, in North Carolina. Sailing up-river some 50 miles to the small town of Bath, Teach appears to have decided to settle down and to abandon his piratical ways. It was at Bath that he bought a house, and according to Johnson in *A General History*, took a young girl as his common-law wife (as mentioned earlier). He also applied for the King's Pardon and this was granted by the governor, Charles Eden. It is far from clear how far the governor was in cahoots with Teach, and certainly some have suggested that the two were close friends at this time. What is known is that Teach quickly became bored with shore-based life, and decided to resume his old career. When he reappeared in the colony with a French merchant ship in tow, he apparently told the governor that she had been found 'abandoned' – albeit with a cargo of sugar. The Vice Admiralty Court which was promptly called by Governor Eden came to the conclusion that the ship was derelict and hastened to award the cargo jointly to Eden (sixty hogsheads of sugar) the President of the Court (twenty hogsheads) and to Teach and his crew (whatever else remained of the cargo). This certainly suggests that an element of corruption and collusion may have been present.

After a brief but boozy reunion off Ocracoke Island with his old cronies 'Calico Jack' Rackam and Charles Vane, Teach and his former colleagues were beginning to alarm the authorities – not just in North Carolina but in Pennsylvania, and Virginia, where law-abiding folk took a dim view of large numbers of former pirates appearing to want to settle in their midst. People had serious doubts about whether the men were complying with the terms of their Pardon, and were not convinced that Governor

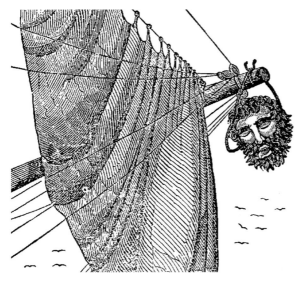

The pirate Blackbeard's head hanging from the bowsprit, an image first appearing in 1837 in the *The Pirates Own Book* by Charles Ellms.

Eden and his cronies were willing to take appropriate enforcement action. In the end it was Governor Spotswood of Virginia who financed what was technically a raid on North Carolina territories. The eventual killing of Teach on 22 November 1718 by Maynard has been described already (Chapter Six). In the aftermath, mass hangings of the captured pirates took place, and the news that Blackbeard, the most infamous pirate of all, had met such a grisly fate at the hands of the authorities (twenty sword lacerations to his body as well as five musket-shot wounds) sent shock waves which rippled throughout the Caribbean territories. Teach is thought to have captured more than forty ships in a career which lasted just over two years, but the manner of his appearance, and his apparent unwillingness to use violence (as opposed to threatening it) ensured his reputation as a heroic and gallant figure.

Howell Davis

Where other pirates prevailed through fear and force, Howell Davis added a more subtle palette, using guile and charm when it suited him. It did not stop him being killed in a bloody gun fight, on land, just eleven months into his piracy career. But in that career he is believed to have captured fifteen ships and amassed a fortune which would nowadays equate to £2 million.

Howell Davis shown in a 1728 woodcut.

His stint as pirate began when he was serving as a mate on board the slaving ship *Cadogan* in July 1718. The ship was under the command of a Captain Skinner. The ship was seized by pirate Edward England, and Skinner was so unpopular that he was allegedly pelted with bottles before being shot by the pirates. England offered Davis the chance to command the *Cadogan* if he agreed to join his gang. He readily agreed, and was ordered by England to take the ship to Brazil, and to dispose of the cargo before selling the ship. In practice his crew mutinied and decided to go to Barbados instead, where Davis was promptly accused of piracy and thrown in prison. Curiously the authorities decided that there was insufficient evidence against him – presumably because the *Cadogan* under his command had not captured any other vessels or stolen any cargo, and none of his crewmen could be persuaded to give evidence against him.

He was released and headed for New Providence in the Bahamas, where he was disappointed to find that Woodes Rogers had already begun his cleaning-up operations. There was no safe harbour there for a pirate, so he sailed off as a crew member aboard the sloop *Buck*, led a mutiny when the ship was off Martinique, and for a while operated off the coast of Cuba and Hispaniola. During this time he was based at Coxon's Hole, on Cuba's east coast, and it proved to be an ideal base from which to launch attacks on trading ships using the narrow channel.

With a crew of thirty-five men he proved to be an able leader who, in general, showed few signs of cruelty. However, he could be ruthless and it was reported that when he captured a fellow Welshman by the name of Richard Jones, the captive declined to sign articles to become a pirate. He was however 'persuaded' to change his mind by Davis, after he ordered the man's leg to be slashed with a sword. Jones was then dangled over the side of the boat until hungry sharks were attracted by the smell of blood in the water. A swift reconsideration followed....

His guile and deception came to the fore when he captured a lightly armed merchant ship. Shortly afterwards, he spotted a much larger prize, a heavily armed French merchant ship. He made out that his two ships were both pirate ships, hanging a large Jolly Roger from the merchant ship he had already captured, and this 'conned' the larger vessel into surrendering without a serious fight.

He then headed across the Atlantic towards the African coast. Off the Cape Verde Islands he was able to seize ship after ship, capturing cargoes of slaves, gold dust and ivory, and in time transferred himself to the *Saint James*. The *Saint James* carried twenty-six guns and was an ideal flagship, until it was later replaced by the thirty-two-gun *Rover* off the Gold Coast of Africa. By then Davis had briefly joined forces with the French pirate Olivier Levasseur. Together they took part in the bombardment of the Royal African Company fort at Bence Island (now the Sierra Leone capital of Freetown), reducing it to rubble and seizing any goods of value. Shortly afterwards they captured the *Bird*, under the captaincy of William Snelgrave. The *Bird* was carrying quantities of claret and brandy, which the pirates consumed liberally in the company of the *Bird*'s crew. They all got gloriously drunk and Snelgrave was later to write that Davis was a man 'who (allowing for the Course of Life he had been unhappily engaged in) was a most generous humane Person'.

At one stage Davis captured an English ship called the *Princess of London* on which a young Bartholomew Roberts, another Welshman, was serving as third mate. The two quickly became firm friends, not least because they shared a language (Welsh) which no one else on board could understand. It is easy to see how Roberts, taken under Davis's wing, went on to become one of the most famous pirates of all time, employing many of the deceptions and ruses used by his mentor.

Arriving at a Royal African Company slaving fort in the Gambia, Davis deceived the commander into thinking that he was a legitimate privateer. The commander was invited to dine on board *Saint James*, only for Davis to take him prisoner, successfully ransoming him for a reputed payment of £2,000.

It was a trick he tried once too often. Arriving at the Portuguese island of Principe, off the African Coast, he posed as a Royal Navy pirate hunter and invited the governor to dinner. By then his ship the *Rover* had been fitted with twenty-seven swivel guns in addition to the thirty-two cannon used in her previous incarnation, when she was known as the Dutch vessel *Marquis del Campo*. The Portuguese suspected a trap and suggested that Davis join the governor for drinks before dinner. How civilised it all sounds! In practice, the Portuguese militia, armed with muskets, laid an ambush and after a bloody fight Davis and seven of his shore party were killed. That same night, on 19 June 1719, Bartholomew Roberts was elected leader of the remaining pirates, took command of the *Rover*, and promptly brought all her guns to bear on the town. That night the town was razed to the ground.

Charming, courteous and cunning, Davis may be one of the lesser-known pirates, but perhaps his greatest legacy was the inspiration and guidance he gave to Bartholomew Roberts, later to become known as Black Bart, or by the Welsh epithet *Barti Ddu*.

John ('Bartholomew') Roberts, aka Black Bart

Born John Roberts in around 1682, probably near Haverfordwest in Wales, this particular pirate was like no other. He was a total abstainer, preferring tea to alcohol. He was strict on discipline – no drinking below deck after lights-out at 20.00 hours. He disapproved of gambling, and the 'no-fighting-on-board-my-ship' rule meant that any disputes had to be settled by a duel – on land.

He adopted the name 'Bartholomew' after becoming a pirate – changing name was not an unusual practice – and it was only after his death that he was given the soubriquet 'Black Bart'.

His success as a pirate was unmatched. He seized well over 400 ships in a brief career which lasted a shade over two years. He was dead by the time he was 40, after having cultivated an image of a smartly dressed if slightly flamboyant captain. Johnson describes him as being black – i.e., with swarthy complexion and dark hair. He was accustomed to appearing on deck in all his finery – wearing a rich damask waistcoat and breeches, with a red feather in his hat. He would wear a gold chain round his neck from which a large diamond crucifix hung down. Sword in hand he was a formidable sight, especially when he stuck two loaded pistols in a silk sash which he draped around his neck and which hung down to his waist.

Before turning to piracy he had worked aboard the slaving ship *Princess* when it sailed from London in 1719, heading for Anamaboe (on Africa's Gold Coast – in what is modern-day Ghana). His capture by Howell Davis has already been described. What is remarkable, especially given his initial reluctance to join the motley crew of Captain Davis, was that when Davis was ambushed and killed, Roberts was elected captain in his place even though at that stage he had only been a pirate for six weeks. Following his decisive destruction of the fort and town at Principe he set off for the Bay of Bahia in Brazil. There, at All Saints Bay, he encountered a fleet of forty-two merchant ships, richly laden, waiting for an armed escort before crossing the Atlantic and the safety of Lisbon harbour. Showing remarkable brio, he attacked and boarded the most heavily laden vessel, the *Sagrada Familia*, capturing a cargo which included 40,000 moidores and a cross of diamonds intended for the Portuguese king.

Dutch and English ships were captured off the Brazilian coast before Roberts moved up to the Caribbean where he harried and looted shipping at will, especially off Barbados and Jamaica. Legitimate trade was brought to a virtual standstill. When the authorities gave chase, he headed north, all the way up to Newfoundland, to find new targets. Before his departure, he was pursued by the *Summerset* and the *Philipa*, operating out of Barbados, and in the ensuing battle, he lost twenty men and incurred considerable damage to his ship the *Fortune*. He limped into harbour at Dominica to carry out repairs but was then set upon by sailors from Martinique.

In retaliation he made a point of being especially harsh in his treatment of any prisoners captured from those islands and he even designed a new flag for himself – with the lettering 'A.B.H.' and 'A.M.H.' (short for 'A Barbadian Head' and 'A Martinican's Head') below a picture of himself standing on two skulls, sword in hand. Johnson tells the story, which is otherwise unsubstantiated, that Roberts at one stage captured the Governor of Martinique and strung him up from the yardarm, by way of revenge for being roughed up. It has to be said that the story may lack any basis in fact – it seems strange that a government official, presumably appointed by the Crown, should be abducted and killed without the French authorities making a great deal of fuss and taking punitive action in revenge. On the other hand, there is a record that a man called Florimund Hurault de Montagny was governor of the island in 1720, and was listed as having died in October that year, cause of death unknown. It is quite possible that Roberts, no lover of authority and with a hatred of Martinique, had a hand in his demise.

After a profitable time off Newfoundland, Roberts returned to the Caribbean, operating in the area around St Kitts, St Barts and St Lucia. Having just about put a stop to all merchant shipping in the area he was forced to look elsewhere. Roberts crossed the Atlantic and kept moving around – Cape Verde Islands, Sierra Leone, and off the coast of modern-day Benin. On one occasion he is alleged to have seized eleven ships in Ouidah harbour and held them to ransom for eight bags of gold dust each. Ten captains paid up, but the eleventh declined. Enraged at such defiance, Roberts set fire to the vessel and allowed it to burn down, notwithstanding the fact that eighty slaves were trapped in the hold. They all perished – either in the flames, or by drowning, or from shark attacks.

In April 1721 Roberts appeared off the Guinea coast in West Africa on his ship *Royal Fortune*, with two other ships, *Ranger* and *Little Ranger*. After a successful mission burning and looting they were spotted by a Royal Navy vessel the *Swallow*. As described in Chapter 4, the *Swallow* lured *Ranger* out into the open off Parrot Island, captured it, and then returned to hunt down the *Royal Fortune*. Johnson paints a picture of an almost Drake-like Captain Roberts, determined to finish his breakfast and refusing to take the imminent attack seriously, until it was far, far too late. His crew meanwhile were paralytically drunk and unable to act in a sensible manner. They had spent the whole of the previous day carousing and celebrating the recent capture of the brigantine *Neptune*. The date: 10 February 1722. In the ensuing mêlée Roberts was struck in the throat by grapeshot, severing his windpipe. His crew somehow managed to implement the captain's oft-repeated desire to be buried at sea, by wrapping his body in a shroud made of a small sail, weighted it and tossed it overboard before the crew of the *Swallow* were able to grab the corpse. The pirate crew either died in action or were captured, and over 250 pirates were subjected to the full rigours of the law, as described on page 49. One interesting aside (and it indicates how willing people are to embroider, fantasise and twist the stories of pirates): the fact that the body of Roberts was never recovered has enabled one author to conjecture that 'his' body was thrown overboard to disguise the fact that 'he' was actually 'she'. With so little substantiated evidence, there will always be room for conspiracy theories and for a twenty-first-century 'take' on eighteenth-century events.

What the intervening years have shown is that never again would a pirate captain command such a large and successful operation. Roberts was ruthless, cruel and a

ABH AMH

Black Bart's flag.

brilliant navigator. He was not the last pirate to menace shipping on both sides of the Atlantic, but he was perhaps the last to do so in such a successful manner that he threatened the whole prosperity of the Caribbean and West African settlements. After his death, ship owners who were seeking quick profits turned from piracy to shipping slaves, and British imperial aspirations changed dramatically. Roberts was one of the last of his generation who tried piracy to make their fortune. The next generation would exploit the demand for slaves throughout the colonies, both in America and the Caribbean. The slaves made huge profits for the sea captains; they also made huge profits for the plantation owners. And both sailors and merchants alike ploughed their fortunes back into Britain's economy.

****

A final sign that times had changed: Captain Gow

If any one case showed how the reality of piracy was different to the sanitised and highly glamorised version put forward by Johnson in his *A General History*, the case of Captain Gow is a fine example. His case was reported not in the *General History* – his piracy exploits occurred a few years after it was published – but in the reports of his Old Bailey trial set out in the *Newgate Calendar*.

Gow, who hailed from the Orkneys, was second mate aboard a merchant ship called the *George,* bound for Santa Cruz. He was elected leader of a group of mutineers who had taken over their ship one night after slitting the throats of the first mate and the ship's surgeon. These unfortunate victims had staggered onto the deck holding their throats, pleading for help, only to be shot at point blank range and tossed overboard. The captain, hearing the commotion, emerged from his cabin, was stabbed twice and turned to Gow to plead for mercy. The trial report shows: '... Gow, who had been assisting in the murders between the decks, came on the quarter-deck and fired a brace of balls into the captain's body, which put a period to his life.'

Gow then renamed the ship *Revenge* and led the men to a series of spectacularly unsuccessful ship seizures. One turned out to contain a cargo of cod from Newfoundland bound for Cadiz, another was stocked with pickled herrings from Scotland destined for Italy (a far cry from the usual tales of pirate's treasure). Worse, the pirates then started to suffer dreadfully from dehydration owing to a shortage of potable water. They ventured down to Madeira but did not dare put ashore for urgently needed supplies for fear of being recognised. They continued to make minor captures of merchant ships – landing yet another vessel packed with salted fish! These captures merely added to the list of prisoners who all needed to be watered and fed. One of the mutineers, by the name of Williams, had an answer for all such problems: slit their throats and throw them overboard. Eventually the crew tired of this bloodthirsty approach, especially when he tried to shoot Gow and threatened to blow up the powder store. They persuaded Gow to put Williams on board a ship bound for Bristol, where he was to be placed in irons and handed over to the authorities.

Ironically, the paths of Williams and Gow were to cross again later – in circumstances which neither could have imagined. Meanwhile, Gow and his men ventured up to the Orkneys, where they had tried to outwit a landowner called Fey. He was already known to Gow. But the canny Mr Fey turned the tables on Gow, capturing him and all of his crew one by one, using guile and deception and with the help of barely half a dozen supporters.

A search of the Revenge revealed a document, written by Gow, consisting of six Articles. According to the Court records: 'It is conjectured, that while they were entangled among the rocks of the Orkney Islands, these articles were hastily drawn up, and arose from their distressed situation'.

They read:

I. *That every man shall obey his commander in all respects, as if the ship was his own, and as if he received monthly wages.*

II. *That no man shall give, or dispose of, the ship's provisions; but every one shall have an equal share.*

III. *That no man shall open, or declare to any person or persons, who they are, or what designs they are upon; and any persons so offending shall be punished with immediate death.*

IV. *That no man shall go on shore till the ship is off the ground, and in readiness to put to sea.*

V.   *That every man shall keep his watch night and day; and at the hour of eight in the evening every one shall retire from gaming and drinking, in order to attend his respective station.*

VI. *Every person who shall offend against any of these articles shall be punished with death, or in such other manner as the ship's company shall think proper.'*

Gow and twenty-seven crew were packed off to London, where they found themselves reunited with Williams. After a short trial Gow, Williams and half a dozen of the main accomplices were convicted and sentenced to death by hanging, while the others were acquitted as it was unclear that they had genuinely consented to the crimes. All the hangings took place simultaneously at the Execution Dock in Wapping on 11 August 1729. According to the trial report:

A remarkable circumstance happened to Gow at the place of execution. His friends, anxious to put him out of his pain, pulled his legs so forcibly that the rope broke and he dropped down; on which he was again taken up to the gibbet, and when he was dead was hanged in chains on the banks of the Thames.

As a contrast to the swashbuckling antics of say, Blackbeard or Sam Bellamy, the Gow case was most marked. There was no treasure, there was no daring escape. There were a number of bloody murders, near-starvation, panic, and incompetence. They stole enough fish to feed an army ('Anyone else on board want an extra portion of fish pie? Nice cod and herring....') but ended up throwing the fish away. Gow was not in the least bit heroic, and nobody at Walt Disney Films has tried to make a film based on his life....

His story was however used a century later by Sir Walter Scott in his historical novel *The Pirate*, but it was to be a tale laced with the romance, heroism and gallantry so totally lacking in the original story.

Part Four

Piracy in Literature and Popular Culture

An illustration in the book by Charles Ellms entitled *The Pirates Own Book*, showing pirates preparing to exchange barrels of rum for slaves.

Chapter 13

Books, Ballads and Plays

Buccaneering has long been a popular subject in English literature, dating back to ballads and pamphlets lauding Sir Francis Drake. These started to appear very shortly after the defeat of the Spanish Armada in 1588, with songs such as 'Sir Francis Drake', otherwise known as 'Eighty eight' with verses such as:

The Queen was then at Tilbury,
What more could we desire-a?
Sir Francis Drake, for her sweet sake
Did set 'em all on fire-a'.

Another naval ballad, from the same time, was called 'The Spanish Armada' and contains the words:

We wil not change owre Credo
For Pope, nor boke, nor bell;
and yf the Devil come himself
We'll hounde him back to hell.

These ballads became popular demonstrations of anti-papist sentiments. Buccaneering was equated with patriotism, with being independent, with standing up to Spain and all-things Catholic. And this idea of associating Drake with patriotic acts, with his seamanship celebrated in verses such as: 'Was't not our Drake whose voyage first of all/ Did girdle round the world's terrestrial ball?' found an echo in the following century. In 1655 England invaded Jamaica, seizing control of the island from Spain and building a new capital at Port Royal. It suited the authorities to associate these acts of aggression with Drake's courageous heroics and in 1659 the London stage saw the production of an opera by William Davenant entitled 'Sir Francis Drake', which was a follow-up to the previous year's offering of 'The Cruelty of the Spaniards in Peru'.

Other ballads and pamphlets celebrated early pirates as robbing from the rich (i.e., the Spanish, the Moors, and other 'enemies') to give to the poor (i.e., the impecunious English tar). It was a sort of 'Robin Hood goes to Sea'. As far back

THE
T R Y A L S

OF

Joseph Dawson,   William Bishop,
Edward Forseith,   James Lewis, and
William May,   John Sparkes.

For several

Piracies and Robberies
By them committed,

IN THE

Company of *EVERY* the Grand Pirate,
near the Coasts of the *East-Indies* ; and
several other Places on the Seas.

Giving an ACCOUNT of their *Villainous*
Robberies and *Barbarities.*

At the Admiralty Sessions, *begun at the* Old-
Baily *on the* 29th *of* October, 1696. *and ended on the* 6th. *of* November.

L O N D O N,

Printed for *John Everingham,* Bookseller, at the *Star* in
Ludgate-street, 1696.

Trial reports were bestsellers, fuelling the public appetite for lurid tales of violence, robbery
and punishment.

as the early 1600s there were songs entitled 'Captain Ward the famous pyrate of the world, and an Englishman born' (sung, apparently, to the tune of 'The king's going to Bulloign'). In the late 1500s John Ward had become an anti-hero, one of the most successful corsairs along the Barbary Coast, harassing Spanish and Turkish interests in the Mediterranean. He was English through and through, but if the populace thought that he was wearing Drake's mantle they were wrong; he converted to Islam and changed from refusing to attack English shipping, to actively pursuing ships belonging to Christian countries, including Britain. He became a sort of bogeyman – someone who had committed apostasy, a heretic who had lost his moral compass. His was a frightening story to a population brought up on highly moralistic stories about right and wrong, in which the bad get punished and the righteous get rewarded. John Ward reversed the process both by growing rich and going unpunished. In real life, he may have been a drunken little man who was given the Islamic name of Yusuf Reis and operated out of Tunis until his death in 1622, but to the English he was a figure who both frightened and fascinated. His actions were considered appalling – and yet songs about him were still appearing in print fifty years after his main achievements, and in 1612, while Ward was still alive, the English dramatist Robert Draborne had written a play entitled *A Christian Turn'd Turk*.

One of Ward's associates was the Dutch pirate Zymen Danseker, aka Simon the Dancer, who died in 1615. Fifty years after the time of his main exploits, ballads were still being printed in his honour, including 'The seaman's song of Dansek the Dutchman, his robberies done at sea' from around 1660.

Few of these early ballads were in any way biographical – they simply reiterated the same tale of wicked pirates murdering innocent people and stealing their money 'in drunkenness and letchery' as the 'Seaman's Song' of 1611 puts it.

The last quarter of the seventeenth century saw the publication of a work which was to prove hugely significant to the story of piracy – written by Alexandre Olivier Exquemelin (also known as Exmelin or Oexmelin, and sometimes as John Esquemeling). He had served as a barber-surgeon on board pirate ships in the Caribbean, and had worked alongside Henry Morgan and was with him when Morgan led the invasion of Panama City in 1671. In all probability Exquemelin had been born in France, but later when he returned to Europe he settled in Holland, and his book *De Americaenshe Zee-Rovers* was first published in Dutch, in 1678. Spanish and German translations swiftly followed and in 1684 not one but two separate translations appeared in English, under the title *The Buccaneers of America*. It was also translated into French and became a considerable commercial success. Extraordinarily, Exquemelin then retired from piracy, studied medicine at

Amsterdam, and qualified as a doctor in 1671. Many years later, in 1697 he returned to the West Indies on board the eighty-four-gun *Sceptre*, under the command of Admiral Bernard de Pointis, and took part in the sacking of Cartagena.

These experiences gave his account a very obvious credibility. There are points he may have exaggerated; he may not always have been as 'centre stage' as the accounts suggest; but for the first time people could read what life was actually like aboard a pirate ship. He was not always complimentary about Morgan, suggesting that he made advances towards a young woman who was the wife of a merchant, and who had been captured at Panama. Exquemelin suggested that Morgan forced his attentions on the reluctant lady. Morgan was outraged and, as already mentioned, sued the English publishers for libel, winning £200 in damages. What the book does is show the brutality and cruelty of pirates towards their victims, especially innocent civilians. It demonstrates that they were clever strategists, good sailors and great opportunists – as well as being vicious criminals indulging in drunken debauchery. They were brave, but they were barbaric to the point of showing utter contempt for human life.

The book highlights the life which Exquemelin lived, first as an indentured servant on the island of Tortuga where he was employed by the French West India Company, and then when he threw in his lot with the buccaneers and sailed with them on numerous raiding expeditions. As the author claimed on the title page, it was an account of 'the Famous Adventures and Daring Deeds of Sir Henry Morgan and Other Notorious Freebooters of the Spanish Main'. It is especially interesting in detailing the way that the pirates made decisions on a democratic basis, in terms of where to sail, what ships to pursue, when to attack and so on. It also showed how food was shared equally 'so that the captain is allowed no better fare than the meanest on board'. Above all, Exquemelin shows a deep and abiding hatred of the Spanish, so much so that it must at times cast some doubt on the accuracy of his observations. It was an anti-Catholic bias which was to permeate much of the piracy literature of the time.

Back in England, various literary works followed in the wake of the totally different experiences of Henry Avery and Captain Kidd. Avery was the subject of speculative accounts as to where he went, and what he had done with his money. These ideas were developed in a play *The successful pirate* produced in 1712. It was written by a man called Charles Johnson (not the same Charles Johnson as the one who wrote *A General History of the Pyrates*, although quite possibly his name was used as an inspiration by the real author). It told the story of Avery as a monarch living in Madagascar, and was little more than a rewrite of earlier stories, but cashing in on the notoriety of Avery.

Stories about Kidd were far more real in the sense that people knew of the trial, they knew of the hanging, and were fascinated by the backstory. The trial accounts had become bestsellers, and the question as to what had happened to the plundered booty captured the imagination. Songs such as the 1701 'Captain Kid's Farewell to the Seas, or, the Famous Pirate's Lament' remained popular for a couple of centuries. This popularised the idea that 'Two hundred bars of gold, and rix dollars manifold' formed part of his treasure; (a 'rix dollar' was the English term for silver coinage used throughout the European continent):

Two hundred bars of gold, while we sailed.
Two hundred bars of gold, while we sailed.
Two hundred bars of gold
And rix dollars manifold
We seiz-ed uncontrolled, while we sailed.

But of course the song had to stress the fact that criminals would get their just desserts:

From Newgate now in carts we must go,
From Newgate now in carts we must go,
From Newgate now in carts
With sad and heavy hearts
To have our due deserts we must go.

***

Some thousands they will flock when we die,
Some thousands they will flock when we die,
Some thousands they will flock
To Execution Dock,
Where we must stand the shock
And we must die.

In the period leading up to the publication of *The General History*, Daniel Defoe had written a number of books on the theme of piracy, mutinies and so on. *Robinson Crusoe* was one – another was *The Life, Adventures, and Piracies of the Famous Captain Singleton* (written in 1720). Defoe was fascinated by piracy because it gave him the chance to explore themes which appealed to him; themes of travel, crime, and of national security. He was clearly interested in the human soul – what made men tick, how did they cope with loneliness, what made them choose good or evil? Defoe had also written *The King of the Pirates* in 1719 and later, on the day that the pirate John Gow went to the gallows, he published the 21,000-word pamphlet *Adventures of Captain John Gow* (1725).

Quite clearly, by the time *A General History* came out, piracy was a popular subject. Johnson describes the book in the preface as a 'vivid and bloodthirsty account of a dozen English and Welsh pirates who had recently been in the news', and concentrated on the lives of just twelve of them. The book contained copperplate illustrations of Blackbeard and Bartholomew Roberts – and a pull-out double page featuring the two female pirates Anne Bonny and Mary Read. The first edition swiftly sold out and second and third editions quickly followed. Another printer, Thomas Woodward, brought out a set consisting of two volumes, in the period 1726 to 1728. Volume Two introduced a number of new pirates to the story, including Thomas Tew, Samuel Bellamy, William Fly and William Kidd. By then the popularity of stories about female pirates meant that Mary Read and Anne Bonny started to get top billing. The first edition shows their exploits described in the frontispiece in small italics:

Their *Policies, Discipline* and *Government,*
From their first RISE and SETTLEMENT in the Island
of Providence, in 1717, to the present Year 1724.
WITH
The remarkable ACTIONS and ADVENTURES of the two Fe-
male Pyrates, *Mary Read* and *Anne Bonny.*

Two years later they were far more prominently displayed:

Their firſt Rɪsᴇ and Sᴇᴛᴛʟᴇᴍᴇɴᴛ iɪ the Iſland of
Providence, to the preſent Time.

With the remarkable Aꞓions and Adventures of the two Female Pyrates

Mᴀʀʏ Rᴇᴀᴅ and Aɴɴᴇ Bᴏɴɴʏ;

Setting aside academic discussions about who was or was not the true author of *The General History,* the fact remains that it revolutionised the story of piracy. It became the acknowledged inspiration for later writers including Sir Walter Scott, Robert Louis Stevenson, J M Barrie, and Sir Arthur Conan Doyle. However, it has to be seen as part of a more general interest in crime and punishment. It simply continued the theme of books such as Captain Alexander Smith's 'A Complete history of the lives and robberies of the most notorious highwaymen' published in 1714. To give it its full title, that book offered:

A complete history of the lives and robberies of the most notorious highwaymen, footpads, shoplifts, & cheats of both sexes, wherein their most secret and barbarous murders, unparalleled robberies, notorious thefts, and unheard-of-cheats are set in a true light and exposed to public view, for the common benefit of mankind.

Readers were excited, appalled and intrigued by these 'real life' tales of crime and criminals.

The public was able to read in the press about pirates and highwaymen alike. As the eighteenth century progressed, more and more column inches were filled with lurid tales about piracy. In particular, as the executions gathered pace in the period 1700 to 1720, the papers were filled with details as they filtered back from overseas: the *Weekly Journal or Saturday's Post* of 26 April noted that fifteen pirates had been hanged in New England. When Bonny and Read were convicted of piracy in 1721 the same paper reported on their trial and on the fact that nine fellow pirates had been hanged:

We have an account from Jamaica, by the Fleet newly arrived, of the Execution at Kingston of nine more persons: also the Tryal and Condemnation of eleven others, two of which were women … the Evidence against whom, deposed, That they were both in Men's Habit, and fought desperately, and that they narrowly escap'd being Murder'd by them.

The same year saw a report in the *Weekly Journal or Saturday's Post* of 26 August that:

About 40 pirates have been brought Home by the Mary, Man of War, from Jamaica, to be try'd here by the Court of Admiralty, because several Masters of Ships are now in London, who have been robb'd by them and who are the proper Evidence for convicting them.

A year later the public were able to read in the *Daily Courant* of 30 July 1722 that forty-one out of fifty-eight prisoners tried for piracy had been convicted and hanged.

The fascinated public could then buy reports of the actual trials – and read about them in the *Newgate Calendar*. It was sub-titled *The Malefactors' Bloody Register*, and was typical of the popularity of 'improving literature' in the eighteenth and nineteenth centuries. Originally it consisted of monthly reports issued by the Keeper in Newgate Prison, but other publishers appropriated the title and added sensationalist biographies about famous criminals such as Dick Turpin and Moll Cutpurse. By 1774 a collected edition running to five volumes was available; the work became incredibly popular and was considered compulsory reading – alongside the *Bible* and *The Pilgrim's Progress*.

Pirate cases reported in the *Newgate Calendar* included those for the trial of John Richardson, charged with the murder of Captain Hartley, piracy and theft. Along with his accomplice Richard Coyle, he was hanged at Execution Docks in 1738. The heading to the report shows where its appeal lay for the general public:

> *The crime of piracy is generally accompanied by murder. Richardson, to both these crimes, added that of swindling. His memory will, with justice, be particularly execrated by our female readers; for it will be found that, through the most consummate hypocrisy, he succeeded in seducing, and then abandoning, several of their sex.*

The actual trial report goes on to show that Richardson was invited to spend Christmas with a Mr Brown, who had

> *three daughters and four maid-servants, all of them very agreeable young women. Richardson made presents of India handkerchiefs to all the girls, and so far ingratiated himself into their favour that in a short time all of them were pregnant.*

On another occasion Richardson seduced first a mother and then her two daughters. Of course, he was not hanged for being a libertine and a scoundrel, but for being a murdering pirate, but the tone of the report would have been guaranteed to produce a frisson of horror, and also excitement, in the minds of women of all ages, up and down the country.

By the 1790s the pirate stories had been adapted to the new hippo-dramas – re-enactmnents on stage, usually accompanied by much horse riding, firing of cannon and derring-do. Hence when the Royal Circus opened for its spring season on Easter Monday 1798, it did so with a performance of *Blackbeard – or the Captive Princess*. It ran for 100 nights before transferring to Covent Garden – where it bombed. The circus phenomenon had started with Philip Astley, and he too regularly put on performances featuring re-enactments of battles, in particular with a performance in 1800 featuring his son John Astley in a drama entitled *The Pirates, or, Harlequin Victor*. Theatre records show that no fewer than seventy-five pirate plays and dramatic performances featuring pirates were performed on London stages in the first three decades of the nineteenth century alone. Theatregoers must have wondered whether playwrights ever wrote about anything else.

In 1814 Lord Byron published *The Corsair*. This melodramatic tale of the pirate captain who risks everything to save the life of a slave in a Turkish harem enjoyed a huge success, selling 10,000 copies on its very first day in print. It has, however, been described as the silliest of Byron's narrative poems and is more about Byron and his character flaws, about an impossible love, and about chivalry, than it is about piracy. Nevertheless, it went on to inspire *Il Corsaro* by Giuseppe Verdi, the overture *Le Corsaire* by Hector Berlioz, and the ballet *Le Corsaire* by Adolphe Adam.

In 1836 Edward Lloyd had brought out a sensationalist book about street robberies entitled *The Most Notorious Highwaymen* – a series of loosely connected biographies of famous criminals and their punishments (usually death). It was so successful that Lloyd rushed out a companion volume called the *History of the Pirates of All Nations*. He described it as a narrative of 'a series of gallant sea-fights, dreadful murders, daring attacks, horrid cruelties and barbarities; also their Debauched and Profligate Manner of Living, places of refuge, &c. &c.'

Much of it was a re-hash of earlier works, expressed in the form of a series of lurid instalments which would be collected week by week. Each instalment cost one penny, and was generally printed on a single sheet of paper, folded and refolded (rather like a road map) so that it ran to eight, or sometimes sixteen, pages. These publications became known as 'penny bloods' because of their violent content, but in time the name evolved into 'penny dreadfuls'. They fed the public's demand for gossip, horror stories and crime journalism. For the writers, stories about piracy 'had it all' and they mined the rich seam for all it was worth.

In 1837 a stationer from Boston called Charles Ellms published a book entitled *The Pirates Own Book*. It became hugely popular and was reprinted on many occasions. It was alternatively published under the title *The Pirates: Authentic Narratives of the Lives, Exploits, and Executions of the World's Most Infamous Buccaneers, including Contemporary Eyewitness Accounts, Documents, Trial Transcripts, and Letters*. This collection of pirate narratives concentrates on the swashbuckling and exciting life led by the eighteenth century buccaneers, and was part of a series of books by Ellms looking at tragedies and excitement on the high seas. Other titles included *Shipwrecks and Disasters at Sea* and *The Tragedy of the Seas* along with the 1842 *Robinson Crusoe's Own Book*.

Alongside these publications, serious writers were producing novels which developed the ideas which Defoe had explored in *Robinson Crusoe*. They looked at the idea of the 'noble savage' and considered the role of the pirate, living on the outside of conventional society, as being 'nasty, brutish and short'. The novel,

The Shipwreck, by S H Burney was published in 1816, followed by Sir Walter Scott's *The Pirate* in 1822. The next year saw James Fenimore Cooper's *The Pilot*, followed in 1833 by Edgar Allan Poe's *M/S Found in a Bottle* and *The Gold-Bug* (published in 1843, with its intriguing tale of buried treasure).

But although all the ingredients were in place, none of these works were either aimed at children, or were suitable to be read by them. Then along came the real game-changer: *Treasure Island*. It was originally to be called *The Sea Cook: A Story for Boys*, and was the result of a rain-filled discussion in Braemar between Robert Louis Stevenson and his stepson. Once he had come up with the idea of Long John Silver, Stevenson then sat down and rattled off the first fifteen chapters in as many days. As he later wrote: '*Treasure Island* came out of Kingsley's *At Last,* where I got the Dead Man's Chest—and that was the seed—and out of the great Captain Johnson's *History of the Notorious Pirates.*' Stevenson admitted that he borrowed other ideas from Poe's *The Gold-Bug*, from R M Ballantyne's *The Coral Island* and from stories written by the author Washington Irving. What Stevenson added was that he aimed the story resolutely at young boys; no women spoiled the story, no girls had to be catered for.

The finished story was initially published in seventeen instalments in a children's publication called *Young Folks*, under the title of *Treasure Island, or the mutiny of the Hispaniola*, from October 1881 through to the end of January 1882. It was then issued in book form in 1883 as *Treasure Island*. The public fell in love with the idea of one-legged pirates, parrots, buried treasure and maps marked with an 'X'. Long John Silver was no murdering thief, he was a larger-than-life rogue, a dangerous charmer. In practice, he was inspired by Stevenson's friend W E Henley, who had had his left leg amputated below the knee, and who managed to get around with the aid of a crutch. After the publication of *Treasure Island*, Stevenson wrote to Henley saying:

> *I will now make a confession: It was the sight of your maimed strength and masterfulness that begot Long John Silver … the idea of the maimed man, ruling and dreaded by the sound, was entirely taken from you.*

Stevenson's stepson Lloyd Osbourne, for whom *Treasure Island* was written, was to say of Henley that he was,

> *a great, glowing, massive-shouldered fellow with a big red beard and a crutch; jovial, astoundingly clever, and with a laugh that rolled like music; he had an unimaginable fire and vitality; he swept one off one's feet.*

The book's effect on the public has been immense. Some fifty film versions of the story have been made in the past 100 years, along with dozens of stage productions, and numerous television versions, mini-series, prequels, sequels and other spin-offs. It has become the quintessential pirate tale, filled with tales of treachery, courage – and treasure. All that was needed was to add a sprinkling of magical nonsense – and you get *Pirates of the Caribbean*. It ends up with very little to do with pirates – and everything to do with entertainment.

The *Pirates of the Caribbean* franchise, owned by the Walt Disney Company, consists of five films released in the period 2003 to 2017. As at January 2015 the first four films in the franchise had grossed $3.7 billion. More recent figures suggest that the five films ran up a total of £1.3 billion in production costs but have taken worldwide box office receipts of $4.5 billion. In addition, the popularity of the films has spawned video games, books and various theme parks throughout the world, including those at Paris, Tokyo and Shanghai. It can certainly be argued that piracy was never as profitable as it is now.

Part Five

THE PRESENT TIME

Chapter 14

Modern Day Treasure Hunting – The Lure of Buried Treasure

Looking at just one of the many stories about Captain Kidd's buried treasure gives us an idea of the problems associated with all the other tales of hidden gold. Just days before he was executed (see Chapter 3) Kidd had written a letter to Robert Harley, the Speaker of the House of Commons, offering to reveal the location of his hidden plunder, which was said to be worth £100,000. The transcript of the letter (modern spelling) is as follows:

Sir,

   The sense of my present Condition (being under Condemnation) and the thoughts of having been imposed on by such as seek my destruction thereby to fulfil their ambitious desires makes me incapable of Expressing myself in those terms as I ought, therefore do most humbly pray that you will be pleased to represent to the Honourable House of Commons that in my late proceedings in the Indies I have lodged goods and Treasure to the value of one hundred thousand pounds, which I desire the Government may have the benefit of, in order thereto, I shall desire no manner of liberty but to be kept prisoner on board such ship as may be appointed for that purpose, and only give the necessary directions and in case I fail therein I desire no favour but to be forthwith Executed according to my Sentence. If your honourable house will please to order a Committee to come to me, I doubt not but to give such satisfaction as may obtain mercy, most Humbly submitting to the wisdom of your great assembly. I am Sir Your Unfortunate humble servant

   Wm Kidd

Harley turned down the offer and Kidd took his secret to the gallows. The hidden location of Kidd's treasure – if it existed – was never found. Was it just a final desperate throw of the dice by a condemned man? Did he really leave a secret map showing the whereabouts of the mysterious 'island in the Indies' in his wife's sewing box – and if so how come it reappeared in the 1930s and has never been seen again? Which Indies – East or West?

What was already known was that Kidd had previously left some of his treasure on Gardiner's Island, in East Hampton, New York, and had deliberately revealed its whereabouts at his trial, hoping to gain some sort of credit from the authorities.

So far as the original cache was concerned it appears that in June 1699, Kidd's sloop appeared off Gardiner's Island. Coming ashore, Kidd encountered the owner of the island, a Mr John Gardiner, along with his wife and family. Kidd reputedly gave a piece of gold cloth to Mrs Gardiner as a gift. Under the watchful eye of John Gardiner, Kidd then buried a number of treasure chests on the beach and announced that he would soon return. A variant of the story is that he said that if the treasure went missing, he would kill all the Gardiners. At a later date Kidd disclosed the burial site and soldiers were sent to retrieve the treasure. When it was dug up, the soldiers prepared two lists of what had been found – basically a chest and box of gold, two boxes of silver, bars of silver, gold dust, Spanish dollars, rubies, diamonds, candlesticks and porringers. One list was taken back to Boston with the treasure and has apparently ended up in the Royal Collection. The other was left with John Gardiner as a receipt and is now held as part of the Long Island Collection of the East Hampton Library. It apparently differs in a number of significant respects from the other copy, suggesting that light fingers may have been at work and that some of the hoard 'disappeared' in transit to the British Government....

But this small amount of treasure recovered by the authorities has been used to suggest that a much larger haul remains buried from view – i.e., the £100,000 referred to by Kidd immediately before his hanging. This idea of a huge treasure was embellished by later writers such as Edgar Allan Poe's *The Gold-Bug*, Washington Irving's *The Devil and Tom Walker*, Robert Louis Stevenson's *Treasure Island* and Nelson DeMille's *Plum Island*.

No matter that there is no suggestion that Kidd ever ventured up to the shores of Nova Scotia, least of all to Oak Island, but the story started to emerge of strange symbols and burial shafts on that island, linked to Kidd. By 1948 a newspaper in Oklahoma called the Lawton Constitution was carrying a story in its edition of 26 August that treasure hunters were:

seeking a nest egg that Captain Kidd is supposed to have planted [on Oak Island].... It all started back in 1796 when 3 boys from the nearby mainland village of Western Shore saw an old ship's block hanging from an oak limb. Beneath it was a depression in the earth about 30 feet in circumference. The boys rowed home to get shovels and started to dig. Ten feet down they struck a floor of oak planks. They found other floors every ten feet down to 90 feet. At 96 feet, water flooded the pit. The boys really started something. For the next 100 years scores of gold-hungry hopefuls continued to dig. Each time they got a shaft down 96 feet water from the underground channel washed them out.

Pausing there, our journalist might have considered exactly what was involved in digging a hole 96 ft deep. No mention of the vast amounts of timber needed to shore up the sides, or the ladders, pulleys, rope and so on needed to bring excavated material to the surface from that depth. No matter that this was 'three boys' on a bit of a lark, at the turn of the eighteenth century.

The article went on to explain that mechanical diggers had recently been brought in by a treasure hunter and that he had discovered 3 chests almost 150 ft down. 'At least, the Nova Scotia Ministry of Trade says he did.' The article also explains that the three shafts, all securely shored up, could still be seen. And the connection with Kidd? Well, 'rumour has it' that there used to be a sign (nobody is sure when or where) reading '200 N' and below it the word 'KIDD'. Hardly the most conclusive scientific proof....

At that point the story starts to unravel with a tale of three travellers who, according to Masonic lore, discover Enoch's Vault of nine descending arches under the ruins of King Solomon's Temple at the bottom of which is the 'Lost Word'. The story unravels further with treasure maps which curiously resemble Juan Fernandez Island (now renamed Robinson Crusoe Island, off the coast of Chile) being transposed onto Oak Island, and with a hoaxer claiming to be the reincarnation of Captain Kidd, going around leaving fake clues linking the island to Kidd's treasure.

The story is set out because it gives some idea of how long hoaxers have been around, and how 'evidence' manufactured a century ago can easily pass for genuine evidence from 300 years ago. It doesn't take a genius to work out that three schoolboys could not possibly have hand-dug a pit 96 ft deep on a sandy island. It also raises suspicions when the same setting is also chosen as a possible hiding place both for Marie Antoinette's missing jewellery, and for treasure buried by the Knights Templar. Some have suggested that it is linked to the Holy Grail and the Ark of the Covenant. Others claim that the massive engineering work must have been the result of French activity during the Seven Years War linked to the fortress at Louisbourg, aimed at hiding the treasures contained in the fort from the advancing British forces.

In other words, it was all hokum built upon nonsense, embroidered with half-truths and laced with pseudo-scientific gobbledegook, administered with a large helping of wishful thinking. And yes, it was in all probability helped along by bored museum archivists, fantasists and fraudsters who thought it would be fun to 'seed' the area with fake clues and forged maps.

What no one seems to have worked out is that it is highly unlikely that Kidd had with him any substantial treasure once he was deserted by the majority of his crew off Madagascar. Is it really likely that the men who deserted him to join Culliford would have left him one penny more than he was strictly entitled to under the terms of their particular code? Is it not much more likely that they kept the lion's share of the money to themselves, leaving Kidd and his dozen or so men with the comparatively small amount of treasure which he deposited on Gardiners Island? It seems far more likely that the fabled treasure seized on the *Quedagh Merchant* made its way into the taverns and bordellos of Madagascar, but that has not stopped successive generations of treasure hunters looking for it in a huge swathe of land from the Caribbean to New York and Nova Scotia. Charles Island, the Thimble Islands and Cockenoe Island (all of them off the coast of Connecticut) have all featured in treasure hunts, no doubt encouraged by local hoteliers and businessmen with a vested interest in bringing tourists to the area. There have also been treasure hunts conducted in Suffolk County, and Long Island in New York and on the island of Grand Manan in the Bay of Fundy (between the Canadian provinces of New Brunswick and Nova Scotia).

Curiously, the 'bones' of the *Quedagh Merchant* may well have been located, in a few metres of water just 20 metres off the coast of Dominica. Kidd is thought to have ordered the boat to be emptied of cargo, set on fire, and then scuttled as a means of hiding his connection to the pirated ship. In 2007 divers announced that they had located a wreck off Catalina Island and believed it to be the remains of the *Quedagh Merchant*. The distribution of some twenty-six cannon, all loaded together in the same part of the ship, is compatible with the idea of a deliberate sinking. The large amount of heavy scrap metal found on board ties in with Kidd's own reports that he had loaded 10 tons of scrap iron as ballast before leaving Madagascar. Archaeologists from Indiana are confident that they will be able to prove conclusively the identity of the wreck, and then preserve it as part of the island's heritage. To that end the wreck site has been designated as a Living Museum in the Sea, effective 23 May, 2011. As such, the *'Naufragio de Capitán Kidd'* is now protected under Dominican Republic law for this and future generations.

Meanwhile, reports that some of Kidd's treasure had been found off Madagascar by American explorer Barry Clifford have turned out to be rather less convincing. Having brought up a 'solid silver bar' weighing 50kg in 2015 Clifford solemnly presented it to the President of Madagascar. Embarrassingly, UNESCO subsequently rubbished the explorer's find, saying that no proper archaeology had been undertaken, and that the jump from 'here is a lump of metal', to 'here is some of Kidd's treasure', was wholly unsubstantiated. Indeed, subsequent tests suggest that the bar contained no silver whatsoever and was ninety-five per cent lead. A more prosaic explanation for it was that it formed part of ballast used when constructing a jetty as part of the island's harbour works.

It is not the first time that Barry Clifford's claims have been poo-pooed by UNESCO. At one stage he claimed to have discovered the flagship of Christopher Columbus, submerged in waters off the northern coast of Haiti, whereas tests later showed that the wreck was from a substantially later period.

On the other hand, credit has to go to Mr Clifford for bringing to the surface vast quantities of treasure associated with 'Black Sam' Bellamy's *Whydah*, first located in 1982. Many of the 200,000 artefacts recovered to date have formed part of a travelling exhibition touring the United States under the auspices of the National Geographic Magazine. And while the headlines may go to the fortune in gold coins, it is the more mundane items which help create a fascinating insight into everyday life aboard a pirate ship at the start of the Georgian era. In 2017 the recovery team announced that they had recovered what is believed to be Bellamy's personal pistol. Alongside the pistol, human bones were discovered and it was announced in 2018 that these were to be sent away for DNA analysis. It is hoped that it can be established beyond doubt that the mortal remains of a most intriguing pirate have been identified.

As for the coins, it helps to know that the silver coins were known as 'reales' (coming in multiples of 1, 2, 4 and 8). The largest reales were often referred to as 'pieces of eight' or 'pesos' (short for pesos de ocho). Sixteen reales had the same value as one escudo – a gold coin which derived its name from the shield comprising the design on the reverse side of the coin. The one escudo coin contained typically 0.8 troy ounces of gold while the 8 reales coin contained 0.8 troy ounces of silver. The two escudos coin was originally known as a 'pistole' but became more generally known as a doubloon, and doubloons were minted not just in Spain but in Peru, Mexico and what was called Nueva Granada – modern-day Ecuador, Panama, and Venezuela. Doubloons were also minted in Portuguese colonies, where they went by the name 'dobrão'. A more generic name for a Portuguese gold coin is a moidore – a corruption of the Portuguese phrase 'moeda d'ouro', meaning 'gold coin'. Moidores in the form of reales – in Portuguese, réis – were used as currency in Portuguese colonies throughout the world, an empire which now translates to over fifty different countries worldwide, from Brazil to Mozambique and from Goa to Macao. Indeed, in the period in which pirates were most active the moidore became the most commonly traded coin in the New World and was internationally the principal gold coin of the eighteenth century. In Britain during the reign of George I, the one moidore coin had a value of twenty-seven shillings. Its design featured the crowned Arms of Portugal on the obverse and the distinctive Cross of Jerusalem on the reverse. In 1722 King John V of Portugal introduced a new gold coin called the escudo, nick-named a 'Joey', but also known as a 'Portuguese Piece' or 'Port Piece' and trading in Britain at the time as being equivalent to nine shillings.

Many of the coins produced in the Spanish colonies were called cobs – hand-struck onto irregular shaped pieces of gold or silver, trimmed by the moneyer to provide for the correct weight. In time these cobs were replaced by milled coinage – where the silver or gold was first made into sheets of uniform thickness, punched out to form blanks known as 'planchets'. These would then be struck in large screw presses, giving a much more uniform imprint than could ever be obtained with the hammers used to make cobs.

You have to think that if there were caches of such coins buried throughout the Caribbean, and on Madagascar and its neighbouring islands, metal detectorists would have found them by now.

As for the treasure scattered in the great storm of 1715 it is believed that the Spanish 'wreck-fishers' recovered over 1¼ million pesos, sufficient to fill the holds of two galleons which were then sent back to Spain to complete their journey. However, this left an estimated quarter-of-a-million pieces of eight scattered over fifty miles of the ocean floor. Few attempts were made in the next 200 years to carry out any serious research and it was not until 1948 that American Kip Wagner discovered Spanish coins on the beach near Sebastien Inlet. Intrigued, he studied old maps of the area, bought a second-hand metal detector for $15, and also chartered a small plane to carry out reconnaissance from the air. Over the years he conducted a treasure hunt which has yielded much in the way of treasure. By the 1960s, divers had recovered more than 4,000 pieces of eight, along with a plethora of artefacts, many of them made of gold and exquisitely fashioned. All the coins which were recovered were cobs, most of them minted between 1711 and 1715 in Mexico City, although all the other colonial mints were represented and coins of earlier dates have also been recovered, some dating back to the 1650s.

It would however be naïve to think that all the treasure had been found and vacuumed up, since the wrecks of two of the largest ships, the *Regla* and the *Santo Cristo* have never been recovered. The *Regla* alone was recorded to be carrying over 8,000 chests and sacks of silver along with sixty chests of gifts and one small chest of gold bars, doubloons and pearls, to say nothing of quantities of other valuables. The *Santa Cristo* is reported to have contained over 2 million pesos, along with 684 chests carrying valuables – everything from porcelain to silver objects. The State of Florida has granted licences for various areas of the ocean floor to be explored, and as sonar and so on becomes more sophisticated it is assumed that further finds will be made.

In particular, inventions designed to help research into mineral deposits, or for salvaging sunken vessels, have been adapted to assist both the land-based and the marine archaeologist. The 'full works' which come under the general umbrella of 'geophysics' includes ground-penetrating radar, sonar, electrical resistance meters, magnetometers and electromagnetic conductivity meters.

There is an unexpected name which appears in the annals of underwater exploration – that of Benito Mussolini. He was one of the first to try and use a metal detector to locate items on the sea bed, or more accurately, the lake bed. In the late 1920s Lake Nemi in Italy was drained in order to give access to two historic pleasure barges, believed to have been constructed during the reign of the

Emperor Caligula (AD 12–24). One was an impressive 250 ft long, and both vessels were expected to reveal a host of information about early shipbuilding techniques. Perhaps it was a case that Mussolini wanted his fascist regime to be associated with the glories of Rome's past – but having located the ships he then wanted to carry out further research and to identify and recover items from the lake floor. He brought in metal detectorist Shirl Herr, an American inventor who was keen to demonstrate his portable machine for locating objects underwater. This was not the very first metal detector, but it was patented in 1924 and proved itself superior to other devices. Herr accompanied Mussolini in an expedition exploring the exposed mud at the bottom of the lake, and located a number of items of lead, iron and gold, now exhibited in various local museums. Ironically, they represent all that remains of the excavations – the ships themselves were destroyed in the Second World War.

Other inventions followed, but there are often problems with using the sensitive equipment in any great depth of water. By 2011 the American firm of Garrett had released its AT Gold metal detector which it claims can operate in up to 10 ft of water. Meanwhile, advances in sonar hydrographic technology have meant that items resting on the seabed can now be identified with amazing clarity. For that reason, further pirate ships are likely to be located, with or without their treasures intact. In the mid-90s, divers off the coast of North Carolina working for a company called Intersal Inc. announced that they had discovered the wreck of the *Queen Anne's Revenge*. Over the intervening period some quarter of a million artefacts have been recovered, including over thirty cannon from a number of different European manufacturers, suggesting that these were gathered from a number of different captured ships. A sword hilt and navigational devices have been recovered, along with 'domestic' items and an anchor weighing well over 1.4 tons. But unlike the *Whydah* galley, nothing conclusively establishes the vessel as the ship on which Edward Teach went to his watery grave, although each diving season's finds make this seem more and more likely.

Another much-hyped tale of buried treasure concerns the treasure of Levasseur. As mentioned in Chapter 11, he allegedly hurled his necklace into the crowd of piratical supporters gathered to watch his execution – and supposedly this contained clues as to where his treasure was buried. There are no records to substantiate this, or to show who caught the necklace, or to establish what the clues were. There is then a gap of two centuries before a woman called Rose Savy, widow of Charles Savy, found carvings on the rocks at Beau Vallon on the Seychelle island of Mahé. This was in 1923. Apparently, no one had noticed these before because it was an exceptionally low tide, but the markings are said to have included carvings of a dog, a snake, a turtle, a horse, two joined hearts, a staring eye and much more besides. It sounds a positive art gallery of stone carvings….

At this point in the story enter 'a notary' (it is always useful to add in a notary to a story – it gives extra credibility), but a century on it is difficult to substantiate

1738 engraving of the Queen
Anne's Revenge.

who this notary was, or why he suddenly came out with the information that he had
found a map of the Beau Vallon area, dated 1735, with the words written on it that
the owner of the land was 'La Buse'. From this he deduced that the rocks were carved
by Levasseur, and were definitely clues to where his treasure was hidden. More
information suddenly appeared in the hands of the notary – including a number of
cryptograms allegedly relating to the treasure. These, it was said, were found with
the testamentary papers of one Bernardin Nageon de L'Estang, nicknamed 'le
Butin', who died seventy years after Levasseur. No one has sought to show how these
cryptograms have any relevance to Levasseur's necklace, or to link in any way to his
treasure. However, it has given a number of enthusiastic codebreakers the chance to
come up with possible solutions. The code requires a knowledge of Masonic beliefs;
it is a rebus and involves the Twelve Labours of Hercules. It mentions the Clavicles of
Solomon and the Signs of the Zodiac – it is a wild goose chase of nonsense.

One particular man seized on the clues and spent many years trying to uncover
the significance of the code, a man by the name of Reginald Cruise-Wilkins. He was
a neighbour of Rose Savy and in 1947 he started a quest which was to occupy him
for the last thirty years of his life. To his way of thinking, he established a number
of things about the treasure: there was a secret chamber somewhere underground
which must be approached carefully, to avoid being flooded. It is protected by the
tides, and is to be approached from the north. Also, the order in which various tasks
have to be undertaken is crucial.

Over the years the original seventeen lines of the cryptogram have been supplemented with another five lines of text, using the same encryption. Interestingly, the Cipher Foundation translates the extra lines as starting off with the words: 'A good drink in the bishop's hostel in the devil's seat…', a direct crib from Edgar Allan Poe's *The Gold-Bug* written in 1843. This suggests that people have been coming up with forged documents, fake directions and planted evidence for rather a long time!

Reginald died in 1977 and his son, John, a history teacher in the Seychelles, is still trying to locate the treasure. By now it has become an engineering project involving building dams and using explosives – and of course in the meantime it has the advantage of keeping the treasure very much in the news, and in the minds of the tourists visiting Mahé. In fairness, over the years one or two items have been dug up which might, or might not, have some connection with earlier inhabitants of Beau Vallon who might, or might not, have been pirates. Let's face it, in the early eighteenth century anyone living on Mahé was likely to be living by their wits, doing a bit of smuggling, a spot of wrecking, the occasional act of piracy. So, if a few pistols, a couple of coins, and even a skull with a gold earring has been found, it is hardly a major breakthrough. However, the myth lives on.

Other sites have other supporters – especially on Île Sainte-Marie. And maybe one day the treasure will emerge from its hiding place – although it has to be said that this is more likely to be because of building works rather than any number of dubious documents, dodgy maps, and mysterious rock carvings.

Islamic calligraphy galleon, 1766, by 'Abd al-Qadir Hisari.

The Big 'What If?'

History is full of what-ifs. What if piracy had not been virtually eradicated from the main trade routes in the eighteenth century? Would Britain's navy have been able to defeat the French if all of its energies (time, money and manpower) had been consumed in a perennial cat-and-mouse battle with robbers on the High Seas? Might we have lost India to Napoleon if Nelson had been posted to the West Indies on anti-piracy duties instead of destroying the French navy off the Bay of Aboukir in 1799?

What if the pirates really had set up a proper government of their own on some of the Caribbean islands, levying a sort of tithe to pay for proper fortifications, enabling them to withstand attack from Royal Navy ships? What if they had been able to get a stranglehold on shipping, using bases from Tortuga to the Bahamas and the Virgin Islands, so that they could effectively have held the plantations to ransom? Might the British have abandoned the colonies as expensive experiments on the other side of the world? Would we ever have been able to encourage settlers to set up home on islands such as Mauritius in the Indian Ocean, or Barbados in the Caribbean, if year after year they had seen the fruits of their labour stolen from under their noses?

It is worth remembering that national attempts at colonisation were not always successful – and that failure was incredibly expensive. When Scotland funded the Darien Scheme in the 1690s (an attempt to settle the area of the Isthmus of Panama), it was such a disastrous failure that Scotland was virtually bankrupted. It was estimated that between a quarter and a half of all money in Scotland at the time was tied up in the venture. When the scheme was finally abandoned in 1700, Scotland had little choice but to agree the Act of Union with England. With this as a precedent, how much determination would the British Government have shown if the harvests on Jamaica had been left unsold and stuck in harbour, for year upon year?

For the first King George, coming to the throne just as piracy was threatening to spiral out of control, it may have seemed to be a brave and controversial decision to grant a royal pardon to the pirates, but it was to prove to be a turning point. Trade was seen as being of paramount importance and nothing, but nothing was allowed to come in the way of it, not even the need to punish criminal acts. George may have been catapulted from the relative obscurity of being leader of the tiny Duchy and Electorate of Brunswick-Lüneburg (i.e. Hanover), but now that he was King of Great Britain and Ireland he had no intention of seeing his nascent colonial empire disappear at the hands of a bunch of robbers. Something dramatic was needed – and whereas granting a pardon may have appeared to be a foolhardy risk, it worked.

If the Caribbean plantations had been unprofitable because they were unable to ship their produce back to Britain, would there have been the massive explosion in slavery used as plantation labour? Would we still have had an emerging middle class made up of merchants grown rich on colonial trade? Would the merchants of Bristol and Liverpool have invested money in building and equipping ships for the slave trade if cargoes had been stolen and ships seized on a regular basis? Probably not.

If, instead of holding Charles Town to ransom for a chest of medicine, Edward Teach had 'done a Henry Morgan' and razed the town to the ground, or robbed and tortured its citizens, as Morgan had done in Panama City, would the British Government have decided it could not afford to police settlements on the other side of the Atlantic? It is an interesting point of conjecture.

Would Britain have spearheaded the Industrial Revolution, driven by the search for new ways to develop trade, boost profits and sell more goods? Would insurance companies have survived if they faced continual claims for lost cargoes? And – on a slightly different note – might the pirate communities have developed into an early social experiment, with a society thriving on democratic principles, albeit linked to criminal activities? We might even have seen a Caribbean mafia, holding the trading world to ransom, a kakistocracy in which the most unscrupulous and criminal elements formed the government.

One very specific 'what if' occurred on 28 July 1718 – the day after Woodes Rogers arrived at the Bahamas. What if, instead of burning a French merchant vessel and 'slipping out the back door' of Nassau harbour, Vane had returned the next day and attacked Rogers when he was vulnerable, while unloading the three vessels he had brought across from Europe? What if, when the pirates on the island of New Providence outnumbered the newly arrived militia by ten to one, they had risen up and attacked the fort where Woodes Rogers planned to hang ten of their number on the morning of 12 December 1718? But that tells us a lot about the pirates – they were so busy living for each day that they never planned for tomorrow – for them there was never going to be a tomorrow, and the idea of planning and organising a serious alternative to colonial rule imposed on the islands by the British Government was unrealistic. Ironically, if they had succeeded in driving Woodes Rogers off the island the future of Britain's colonial empire could have been very different.

Clearly it cannot be claimed that Britain's dominance in the world during the period up to the First World War was pinned wholly on her efforts to eradicate piracy. And yet, it played its part. The control of piracy was achieved because rulers were realistic enough to understand that a general pardon was needed, to act as a carrot – just as much as a death penalty and local courts were needed to act as a stick.

The solution was never going to be entirely sea-based – the navy was never going to be large enough to cope with thousands of petty (and not so petty) criminal acts. Similarly, an entirely land-based solution, led by the judiciary and an armed militia, would never be able to impose the Rule of Law throughout such a disparate and far-flung empire. Both approaches were needed – as one suspects is still the case today with the recurring problems with piracy off the coast of Somalia.

Without a proper government in place in Somalia, without an independent judiciary and police force, any number of patrol boats at sea will not be able to rid an area of fast-moving pirate boats intent on seizing and holding to ransom unarmed tankers, tourist yachts, and so on. And just as 300 years ago, when much of the piracy was borne out of injustice – especially at the way seamen were treated aboard both merchant and Royal Navy ships, so the world will need to come to address the legitimate grievances of the Somali fishermen, whose seas have been polluted by neighbouring countries, whose fish stocks have been depleted by uncontrolled foreign intervention, and who find themselves unable to sustain their families. That is not to excuse organised crime syndicates, warlords and murderous thieves, but a recognition that piracy in its widest sense – stealing property on the High Seas – has always been with us, and probably will always remain.

Appendix 1

Letter of Appointment and instructions to Sir Henry Morgan from Thomas Modyford (modern spelling):

To Admiral Henry Morgan, Esq. Greeting.
Whereas the Queen Regent of Spain hath by her Royal Shadula, [i.e. Decree] dated at Madrid the 20th of April, 1669, Commanded her respective Governors in the Indies to publish and make War against our Sovereign Lord the King in these Parts.;And Whereas Don Pedro Bayona de Villa Nueva, Captain General of the Province of Paraguay and Governor of the City of St. Jago de Cuba and its Provinces, hath executed the same, and lately in the most hostile and barbarous manner landed his men on the north side of this Island, and entered a small way into the Country, firing all the Houses they came at, killing or taking Prisoners all the Inhabitants they could meet with; and whereas the rest of the Governors in these Parts have granted Commissions for executing the like Hostility against us, and are diligently gathering Forces together to be sent to St Jago de Cuba, their General Rendezvous and place of Magazine, and from thence as the most opportune place to be transported for a thorough Invasion and final Conquest (as they hope) of this Island, for the prevention of which their mischievous Intentions, in discharge of the great trust which His Gracious Majesty hath placed in me, I do by virtue of full Power and Authority in such cases from His Royal Highness, James Duke of York, His Majesties Lord High Admiral, derived unto me, and out of the great confidence I have in the good conduct, courage, and fidelity of you the said Henry Morgan to be Admiral and Commander in chief of all the Ships, Barques, and other Vessels now fitted, or which hereafter shall be fitted for the public Service and defence of this Island, and also of the Officers, Soldiers, and Seamen, which are, or shall be put upon the same, requiring you to use your best endeavours to get the vessels into one Body or Fleet, and to cause them to be well manned, fitted, armed, and victualled, and by the first opportunity, wind and weather permitting, to put to Sea for the Guard and Defence of this island, and of all vessels trading to or about the same; and in order thereunto to use your best endeavours to surprise, take, sink, disperse, and destroy all the enemies ships

or vessels which shall come within your view, and also for preventing the intended Invasion against this place, you are hereby further authorised and required, in the case that you and your Officers in your Judgement find it possible, or feasible to land and attain the said Town of St Jago de Cuba, or any other place belonging to the Enemies, where you shall be informed that Magazines and Stores for this War are laid up, or where any Rendezvous for their Forces to embody are appointed and there to use your best endeavours for the seizing the said Stores, and to take, kill, and disperse the said Forces.

And all Officers, Soldiers, and Seamen, who are or shall be belonging to or embarked upon the said vessels are hereby strictly enjoined both by Sea and Land, to obey you as their Admiral and Commander in chief of in all things as be cometh them; and you yourself are to observe and follow all such Orders as you shall from time to time received from His most excellent Majesty, his Royal Highness, or myself.

In addition to the above a separate list of instructions were delivered to

Admiral Henry Morgan, Esq. the 22nd of July, 1670, together with his Commission.

1   *You will with these Instructions receive my Commission which you are enjoined with all expedition to publish and put in due execution, according to the full extent and import of the same, for the accomplishing whereof, you shall have all the assistance this Island can give you*

2   *You are to make known to me what strength you can possibly make, what your wants may be, that on due calculation of both, we may supply you with all possible speed*

3   *You are to take notice and advise your Fleet and Soldiers that you are on the old pleasing Account of no purchase no pay, and therefore that all which is got shall be divided amongst them according to accustomed Rules*

4   *In case you shall find it prudential as by your Commission you are directed, to attain St Jago de Cuba, and God blessing you with victory, you are hereby directed, in case you do it without any considerable hazards, to keep and make good the place and country thereabout, until you have advised me of your success and received my further Orders touching the same, lest your suddenly quitting and their suddenly returning, beget us new work, and put on new charges and hazards for the second defeating*

5   *In order to do this you are to proclaim mercy and enjoyment of estates and liberty of customs to all the Spaniards that will submit and give assurance*

of their Loyalty to His Majesty, and Liberty to all the Slaves that will come in; and to such as by any good service may deserve the same; you are to give notice that their fugitive Masters' Plantations are to be divided amongst them as rewards for the same & make them sufficient Grants in writing, both for their Liberties and Estates, reserving to the Crown of England the fourth part of the produce to be yearly paid for the yearly maintenance of such Forces as shall defend those parts

6 *In case you find that course to take approvable effect, you are as much as will stand with the same to preserve the Sugar-works and Canes; but if it otherwise appear to you, that in reason you cannot make good the place for any long time, and that the Spaniards and Slaves are deaf to your Proposals, you are then, with all it as a Wilderness, putting the Men-Slaves to the Sword and making the Women-Slaves Prisoners to be brought hither, and sold for the account of your Fleet and Army, such of the men also that cannot speak Spanish, or any new Negro, you may preserve for the same account; or if any Ships to be present to carry them for New England or Virginia, you may send them all on the same account*

7 *You are to enquire what usage our Prisoners have had, and what Quarter hath been given by the Enemy to such of ours as have fallen under their power, and being well informed, you are to give the same, or rather as our custom is to exceed in Civility and Humanity, endeavouring by all means to make all sorts of People sensible of your Moderation and good nature, and your inaptitude and loathing to spill the blood of men*

8 *You have hereby power to execute Martial Law, according to such military Laws as have been made by me, and the Laws made by Act of Parliament for the government of the Fleet, which I approve of as fitting for the Service; and hereby authorise you to put them in execution against such as shall offend you, having first published the Laws unto them, that none may pretend ignorance*

9 *If any Ship or Ships shall be present, which have not any Commissions, you are hereby empowered to Grant Commissions to them according to the form I have used, taking security of £1,000 for the performance of the same.*

10 *What Ships in this Expedition you shall keep with you under your Command and them order and dispose for the best improvement of this Service, not suffering the takers or pretenders to sell them until they come into their Commission Port*

11   *In regard many things may happen in this Action which cannot be by me foreseen and provided for in these Instructions, therefore all such matters are left to your well known prudence and conduct, referring to you that are in the place to do therein what shall be needful, thus wishing you success and this Island made happy thereby, I remain your faithful Friend and Servant Thos. Modyford*

Appendix 2

To give an idea of the style and content of the book *A General History of the Pyrates*, this is an extract from its description of Blackbeard's final days, shown courtesy of Project Gutenberg:

Blackbeard the Pirate

Lieutenant *Maynard* came to an Anchor, for the Place being shoal, and the Channel intricate, there was no getting in, where *Teach* lay, that Night; but in the Morning he weighed, and sent his Boat a-head of the Sloops to sound; and coming within Gun-Shot of the Pyrate, received his Fire; whereupon *Maynard* hoisted the King's Colours, and stood directly towards him, with the best Way that his Sails and Oars could make. *Black-beard* cut his Cable, and endeavoured to make a running Fight, keeping a continual Fire at his Enemies, with his Guns; Mr *Maynard* not having any, kept a constant Fire with small Arms, while some of his Men laboured at their Oars. In a little Time *Teach*'s Sloop ran a-ground, and Mr *Maynard*'s drawing more Water than that of the Pyrate, he could not come near him; so he anchored within half Gun-Shot of the Enemy, and, in order to lighten his Vessel, that he might run him aboard, the Lieutenant ordered all his Ballast to be thrown over-board, and all the Water to be staved, and then weigh'd and stood for him; upon which *Black-beard* hail'd him in this rude Manner: *Damn you for Villains, who are you? And, from whence came you?* The Lieutenant made him Answer, *You may see by our Colours we are no Pyrates. Black-beard* bid him send his Boat on Board, that he might see who he was; but Mr *Maynard* reply'd thus; *I cannot spare my Boat, but I will come aboard of you as soon as I can, with my Sloop.* Upon this, *Black-beard* took a Glass of Liquor, and drank to him with these Words: *Damnation seize my Soul if I give you Quarters, or take any from you.* In Answer to which, Mr *Maynard* told him, *That he expected no Quarters from him, nor should he give him any.*

By this time *Black-beard*'s Sloop fleeted, as Mr *Maynard*'s Sloops were rowing towards him, which being not above a Foot high in the Waste, and consequently the Men all exposed, as they came near together, (there being hitherto little or no Execution done, on either Side,) the Pyrate fired a Broadside, charged with all Manner of small Shot. —A fatal Stroke to them! The Sloop the Lieutenant was in, having twenty Men killed and wounded, and the other Sloop nine. This could not be help'd, for there being no Wind, they were oblig'd to keep to their Oars, otherwise the Pyrate would have got away from him, which, it seems, the Lieutenant was resolute to prevent.

After this unlucky Blow, *Black-beard*'s Sloop fell Broadside to the Shore; Mr *Maynard*'s other Sloop, which was called the *Ranger*, fell a-stern, being, for the present, disabled; so the Lieutenant finding his own Sloop had Way, and would soon be on Board of *Teach*, he ordered all his Men down, for fear of another Broadside, which must have been their Destruction, and the loss of their Expedition. Mr *Maynard* was the only Person that kept the Deck, except the Man at the Helm, whom he directed to lye down snug, and the Men in the Hold were ordered to get their Pistols and their Swords ready for close fighting, and to come up at his Command; in order to which, two Ladders were placed in the Hatch-Way for the more Expedition. When the Lieutenant's Sloop boarded the other, Captain *Teach*'s Men threw in several new fashioned sort of Grenadoes, *viz.* Case Bottles fill'd with Powder, and small Shot, Slugs, and Pieces of Lead or Iron, with a quick Match in the Mouth of it, which being lighted without Side, presently runs into the Bottle to the Powder, and as it is instantly thrown on Board, generally does great Execution, besides putting all the Crew into a Confusion; but by good Providence, they had not that Effect here; the Men being in the Hold, and *Black-beard* seeing few or no Hands aboard, told his Men, *That they were all knock'd on the Head, except three or four; and therefore, says he, let's jump on Board, and cut them to Pieces.*

Whereupon, under the Smoak of one of the Bottles just mentioned, *Black-beard* enters with fourteen Men, over the Bows of *Maynard*'s Sloop, and were not seen by him till the Air cleared; however, he just then gave a Signal to his Men, who all rose in an Instant, and attack'd the Pyrates with as much Bravery as ever was done upon such an Occasion: *Black-beard* and the Lieutenant fired the first Pistol at each other, by which the Pyrate received a Wound, and then engaged with Swords, till the Lieutenant's unluckily broke, and stepping back to cock a Pistol, *Black-beard*, with his Cutlash, was striking at that Instant, that one of *Maynard*'s Men gave him a terrible Wound in the Neck and Throat, by which the Lieutenant came off with a small Cut over his Fingers.

They were now closely and warmly engaged, the Lieutenant and twelve Men, against *Black-beard* and fourteen, till the Sea was tinctur'd with Blood round the Vessel; *Black-beard* received a Shot into his Body from the Pistol that Lieutenant *Maynard* discharg'd, yet he stood his Ground, and fought with great Fury, till he received five and twenty Wounds, and five of them by Shot. At length, as he was cocking another Pistol, having fired several before, he fell down dead; by which

Time eight more out of the fourteen dropp'd, and all the rest, much wounded, jump'd over-board, and call'd out for Quarters, which was granted, tho' it was only prolonging their Lives for a few Days. The Sloop *Ranger* came up, and attack'd the Men that remain'd in *Black-beard*'s Sloop, with equal Bravery, till they likewise cry'd for Quarters.

Here was an End of that couragious Brute, who might have pass'd in the World for a Heroe, had he been employ'd in a good Cause; his Destruction, which was of such Consequence to the Plantations, was entirely owing to the Conduct and Bravery of Lieutenant *Maynard* and his Men, who might have destroy'd him with much less Loss, had they had a Vessel with great Guns; but they were obliged to use small Vessels, because the Holes and Places he lurk'd in, would not admit of others of greater Draught; and it was no small Difficulty for this Gentleman to get to him, having grounded his Vessel, at least, a hundred times, in getting up the River, besides other Discouragements, enough to have turn'd back any Gentleman without Dishonour, who was less resolute and bold than this Lieutenant. The Broadside that did so much Mischief before they boarded, in all Probability saved the rest from Destruction; for before that *Teach* had little or no Hopes of escaping, and therefore had posted a resolute Fellow, a Negroe whom he had bred up, with a lighted Match, in the Powder-Room, with Commands to blow up when he should give him Orders, which was as soon as the Lieutenant and his Men could have entered, that so he might have destroy'd his Conquerors: and when the Negro found how it went with *Black-beard*, he could hardly be perswaded from the rash Action, by two Prisoners that were then in the Hold of the Sloop.

What seems a little odd, is, that some of these Men, who behaved so bravely against *Black-beard*, went afterwards a pyrating themselves, and one of them was taken along with *Roberts*; but I do not find that any of them were provided for, except one that was hanged; but this is a Digression.

The Lieutenant caused *Black-beard*'s Head to be severed from his Body, and hung up at the Bolt-sprit End, then he sailed to *Bath-Town*, to get Relief for his wounded Men.

...

After the wounded Men were pretty well recover'd, the Lieutenant sailed back to the Men of War in *James River*, in *Virginia*, with *Black-beard*'s Head still hanging at the Bolt-sprit End, and fifteen Prisoners, thirteen of whom were hanged. It appearing upon Tryal, that one of them, *viz. Samuel Odell*, was taken out of the trading Sloop, but the Night before the Engagement. This poor Fellow was a little unlucky at his first entering upon his new Trade, there appearing no less than 70 Wounds upon him after the Action, notwithstanding which, he lived, and was cured of them all. The other Person that escaped the Gallows, was one *Israel Hands*, the Master of *Black-beard*'s Sloop, and formerly Captain of the same, before the *Queen Ann's Revenge* was lost in *Topsail* Inlet.

The aforesaid *Hands* happened not to be in the Fight, but was taken afterwards ashore at *Bath-Town*, having been sometime before disabled by *Black-beard*, in one of his savage Humours, after the following Manner.—One Night drinking in his Cabin with *Hands*, the Pilot, and another Man; *Black-beard* without any Provocation privately draws out a small Pair of Pistols, and cocks them under the Table, which being perceived by the Man, he withdrew and went upon Deck, leaving *Hands*, the Pilot, and the Captain together. When the Pistols were ready, he blew out the Candle, and crossing his Hands, discharged them at his Company; *Hands*, the Master, was shot thro' the Knee, and lam'd for Life; the other Pistol did no Execution. —Being asked the meaning of this, he only answered, by damning them, that *if he did not now and then kill one of them, they would forget who he was.*

Hands being taken, was try'd and condemned, but just as he was about to be executed, a Ship arrives at *Virginia* with a Proclamation for prolonging the Time of his Majesty's Pardon, to such of the Pyrates as should surrender by a limited Time therein expressed: Notwithstanding the Sentence, *Hands* pleaded the Pardon, and was allowed the Benefit of it, and is alive at this Time in London, begging his Bread.

Now that we have given some Account of *Teach*'s Life and Actions, it will not be amiss, that we speak of his Beard, since it did not a little contribute towards making his Name so terrible in those Parts.

Plutarch, and other grave Historians have taken Notice, that several great Men among the *Romans*, took their Sir-Names from certain odd Marks in their Countenances; as *Cicero*, from a Mark or Vetch on his Nose; so our Heroe, Captain *Teach*, assumed the Cognomen of *Black-beard*, from that large Quantity of Hair, which, like a frightful Meteor, covered his whole Face, and frightened *America* more than any Comet that has appeared there a long Time.

This Beard was black, which he suffered to grow of an extravagant Length; as to Breadth, it came up to his Eyes; he was accustomed to twist it with Ribbons, in small Tails, after the Manner of our Ramilies Wiggs, and turn them about his Ears: In Time of Action, he wore a Sling over his Shoulders, with three brace of Pistols, hanging in Holsters like Bandaliers; and stuck lighted Matches under his Hat, which appearing on each Side of his Face, his Eyes naturally looking fierce and wild, made him altogether such a Figure, that Imagination cannot form an Idea of a Fury, from Hell, to look more frightful.

If he had the look of a Fury, his Humours and Passions were suitable to it; we shall relate two or three more of his Extravagancies, which we omitted in the Body of his History, by which it will appear, to what a Pitch of Wickedness, human Nature may arrive, if it's Passions are not checked.

In the Commonwealth of Pyrates, he who goes the greatest Length of Wickedness, is looked upon with a kind of Envy among them, as a Person of a more extraordinary Gallantry, and is thereby entitled to be distinguished by some Post, and if such a one has but Courage, he must certainly be a great Man. The Hero of whom we are writing, was thoroughly accomplished this Way, and some of his Frolicks of Wickedness, were so extravagant, as if he aimed at making his Men believe he was a Devil incarnate; for being one Day at Sea, and a little flushed with drink:—*Come*, says he, *let us make a Hell of our own, and try how long we can bear it*; accordingly he, with two or three others, went down into the Hold, and closing up all the Hatches, filled several Pots full of Brimstone, and other combustible Matter, and set it on Fire, and so continued till they were almost suffocated, when some of the Men cried out for Air; at length he opened the Hatches, not a little pleased that he held out the longest.

The Night before he was killed, he set up and drank till the Morning, with some of his own Men, and the Master of a Merchant-Man, and having had Intelligence of the two Sloops coming to attack him, as has been before observed; one of his Men asked him, in Case any thing should happen to him in the Engagement with the Sloops, whether his Wife knew where he had buried his Money? He answered, *That no Body but himself and the Devil, knew where it was, and the longest Liver should take all.*

Those of his Crew who were taken alive, told a Story which may appear a little incredible; however, we think it will not be fair to omit it, since we had it from their own Mouths. That once upon a Cruize, they found out that they had a Man on Board more than their Crew; such a one was seen several Days among them, sometimes below, and sometimes upon Deck, yet no Man in the Ship could give an Account who he was, or from whence he came; but that he disappeared little before they were cast away in their great Ship, but, it seems, they verily believed it was the Devil.

One would think these Things should induce them to reform their Lives, but so many Reprobates together, encouraged and spirited one another up in their Wickedness, to which a continual Course of drinking did not a little contribute; for in *Black-beard*'s Journal, which was taken, there were several Memorandums of the following Nature, sound writ with his own Hand.— *Such a Day, Rum all out:—Our Company somewhat sober:—A damn'd Confusion amongst us!—Rogues a plotting;—great Talk of Separation.—So I look'd sharp for a Prize;—such a Day took one, with a great deal of Liquor on Board, so kept the Company hot, damned hot, then all Things went well again.*

Thus it was these Wretches passed their Lives, with very little Pleasure or Satisfaction, in the Possession of what they violently take away from others, and sure to pay for it at last, by an ignominious Death.

Bibliography

Adamson, Roger, *Britain's Battle Against Piracy in the Americas in the Early 18th Century*. Illinois Wesleyan University, available online at http://digitalcommons. iwu.edu/cgi/viewcontent.cgi?article=1000&context=history_honproj.

Barrie, J.M., *Peter Pan* [more accurately, *Peter and Wendy*]. London, Hodder & Stoughton, 1911.

Cordingly, David, *Spanish Gold: Captain Woodes Rogers and the True Story of the Pirates of the Caribbean*. London, Bloomsbury Publishing, 2011

Cordingly, David, *Life among the pirates*. London, Little, Brown & Co, 1995

Defoe, Daniel, *The King of the Pirates*. London, A. Bettesworth, 1720

Ellms *Charles, The Pirates Own Book*. Boston, Sanborn and Carter, 1837 and available as a Project Gutenberg e-book at https://www.google.co.uk/ search?q=Ellms,+Charles%3A+The+Pirates+Own+Book.+1837&ie=&oe=

Exquemelin, Alexander O., *The Buccaneers of America,* trans. Alexis Brown. London, W. Crook, 1684; reprint, Mineola, NY, Dover Publications Inc., 2000

Gay, John, *Polly: an Opera*. London, T. Thomas, 1729

Grose, Francis, *Dictionary of the Vulgar Tongue*. London, S Hooper, 1785. Various reprints and available on-line at: https://books.google.es/booksid=4HoSAAA AIAAJ&printsec=frontcover&dq=Grose,+Francis:+Dictionary+of+the+ Vulgar+Tongue,+London,+1785&hl=es&sa=X&ved=0ahUKEwj32LbIjt LUAhVI7BQKHdyaCncQ6AEIJjAA#v=onepage&q&f=false

Halliwell, James Oliver, *The Early Naval Ballads of England*. London, The Percy Society, 1841

Jameson, John Franklin, *Privateering and Piracy in the Colonial Period – Illustrative documents*. New York, the Macmillan Company, 1923. Also available via Project Gutenberg at http://www.gutenberg.org/files/24882/24882-h/24882-h.htm

Johnson, Captain Charles, *A General History of The Robberies and Murders of The Most Notorious Pyrates*. London, Bible and Crown, 1724. Reprint, Mineola, NY: Dover Publications Inc., 1999

Johnson, Samuel, *Political Tracts, the Falklands*. Dublin 1777. Also available as an e-book at https://books.google.es/booksid=dBZgAAAAcAAJ&pg=PA72&lpg =PA72&dq=samuel+johnson+pirates&source=bl&ots=I0AD9kXGjd&sig= DgpjR4ukx5X9RiufH04sGrUNwPk&hl=en&sa=X&ved=0ahUKEwiVm

97C79XUAhXFuhoKHXh6ChAQ6AEIQDAF#v=onepage&q=samuel%20johnson%20pirates&f=false

Lincoln, Margarette, *British Pirates and Society, 1680–1730*. London & New York, Ashgate Publishing, 2014

Powell, M, *British Pirates in Print and Performance*. Palgrave Macmillan, New York, 2015

Privateering and Piracy in the Colonial Period – Illustrative Documents. New York: The Macmillan Company, 1923, and available as a Project Gutenberg e-book at http://www.gutenberg.org/files/24882/24882-h/24882-h.htm

Rediker, Marcus, *Between the Devil and The Deep Blue Sea: Merchant Seamen, Pirates, and the Anglo-American Maritime World, 1700–1750*. Cambridge, University of Cambridge Press, 2003

Riley, Sandra, *Homeward Bound: A History of the Bahama Islands to 1850*. Miami, Florida, 1983

Rogers, Captain Woodes, *A Cruising Voyage Round The World*. London: Printed for A. Bell and B. Lintot, 1712. Reprint, London: Cassell & Co. Ltd., 1923

Snelgrave, William, *A New Account of Some Parts of Guinea and the Slave-Trade*. London, The Crown, 1734. Reprint, London: Frank Cass and Co. 1971

Spotswood, Alexander, *Official Letters in the collections of the Virginia Historical Society* – available via the Library of Congress as a pdf at https://memory.loc.gov/service/gdc/lhbcb/05713/05713.pdf

Stevenson, Robert Louis: *Treasure Island*. London, Cassell & Co. Ltd., 1883

Thomas, Graham. A., *Pirate Hunter – The Life of Captain Woodes Rogers*. Barnsley, Pen and Sword Books, 2008

Trott, Nicholas, *The Tryals of Major Stede Bonnet and other Pirates*. London, Benjamin Cowes, 1719

Wagner, Kim: *Pieces of Eight*. CreateSpace Independent Publishing Platform, 2013

Woodward, Colin, *The Republic of Pirates: Being the True and Surprising Story of the Caribbean Pirates and the Man Who Brought Them Down*. Boston, Houghton Mifflin Harcourt 2008

Websites:

'Pirates and Privateers' hosted by Cindy Vallar: http://www.cindyvallar.com/pirates.html

Colonies Ships and Pirates hosted by David Fictum: https://csphistorical.com/

The Law Library of Congress (for digitised versions of numerous piracy trials etc): https://www.loc.gov/law/help/piracy/piracy_trials.php

Adamson '04, Roger, 'The Fading Gleam of a Golden Age: Britain's Battle Against Piracy in the Americas in the Early 18th Century' (2004).Honors Projects. Paper 21. http://digitalcommons.iwu.edu/history_honproj/21

Accreditation for Images Used

My sincere thanks to all the museums, libraries, galleries and individuals who have allowed the reproduction of images throughout this book.

Image 1
Page vii: Edward Teach in a woodcut from the 1724 book *A General History of the Pyrates*.

Image 2
Page 1: Spanish Galleon, via Wikipedia. Public domain.

Image 3
Page 3: Frontispiece from first edition *A General History of the Pyrates, 1724*. Public domain.

Image 4
Page 8: Bonne's Map of Madagascar from 1770. Public domain.

Image 5
Page 11: Hanging scene: paper cut-out by Richard Hall, c. 1780. Author's private collection.

Image 6
Page 13: Multiple hanging scene by Thomas Rowlandson, date unknown. Public domain.

Image 7
Page 16: Stede Bonnet, from a woodcut taken from *A General History of the Pyrates*.

Image 8
Page 31: Henry Morgan before Panama – engraving used in the 1736 edition of the General History. Public domain.

Image 9
Page 35: Emanuel Bowen's Map of the West Indies, shown courtesy of the Library of Congress.

Image 10
Page 45: A woodcut from *A General History of the Pyrates* (1725). Public domain.

Image 11
Page 47: Port scene: paper cut out by Richard Hall, c. 1780. Author's private collection.

Image 12
Page 54: Thomas Rowlandson (1756–1827), Royal Navy Cook. Wikimedia. Public domain.

Images 13 and 14
Page 65: '*An exact draught of the island of New Providence one of the Bahama Islands in the West Indies*'. [after 1700] Map. Retrieved from the Library of Congress, www.loc.gov/item/74692182. Public domain.

Image 15
Page 69: Military and naval scene: paper cut out by Richard Hall, c. 1780. Author's private collection.

Image 16
Page 71: 36 pounder cannon at the ready, by Antoine Léon Morel-Fatio. Public domain.

Image 17
Page 75: vessels ('Échouage des corvettes dans le Canal Mauvais.') by Louis Le Breton. Copy from the heritage library of Gray, Haute-Saône, France.

Image 18
Page 77: The Sailmaker, Yves Marie Le Gouaz. Shown courtesy of the Rijkmuseum.

Image 19
Page 79: Eighteenth-century engraving of Edward England taken from 'The pirate ship 1660–1730', by Angus Konstam & Tony Brian. Public domain.

Image 20
Page 96: Eighteenth-century woodcut of Edward England (public domain).

Image 21
Page 97: Early eighteenth-century engraving of Charles Vane. Public domain.

Image 22
Page 104: The Hanging of Major Stede Bonnet: an engraving published in the Dutch version of Charles Johnson's *A General History of the Pyrates* in 1725. Public domain.

Image 23
Page 105: Flag of Olivier Levasseur, by 'The Last Brunnen G' (Creative Commons Attribution–Share Alike 4.0 International license).

Image 24
Page 109: Levasseur cryptogram from 'Cryptogramme du Forban trouvé à l'île Mahé'. Public domain.

Image 25
Page 110: Eighteenth-century woodcut of Calico Jack Rackham. Public domain.

Image 26
Page 118: Ann Bonny – engraving first appearing in the Dutch version of Charles Johnson's *A General History of the Pyrates* in 1725. Public domain.

Image 27
Page 119: Mary Read – eighteenth-century engraving. (Wikipedia, Creative Commons Attribution–Share Alike 4.0 International license).

Image 28
Page 119: '*Ann Bonny and Mary Read convicted of piracy*'. Retrieved from the Library of Congress, www.loc.gov/item/2003689011. Public domain.

Image 29
Page 122: Illustration taken from the 1837 *Pirates Own Book* by Charles Ellms. Public domain.

Image 30
Page 123: Captain Howell Davis – illustration from 'A General History of the Pyrates' by Captain Charles Johnson c. 1728.

Image 31
Page 128: Flag of pirate Bartholomew Roberts by 'Orem'. Wikipedia, Creative Commons Attribution–Share Alike 3.0 Unported license.

Image 32
Page 131: Illustration taken from the 1837 *Pirates Own Book* by Charles Ellms. Public domain.

Image 33
Page 133: Trial Reports from 1696. Public domain.

Images 34 and 35
Page 137: Extracts from frontispieces from different editions of *The General History of the Pyrates.*

Image 36
Page 151: Queen Anne's Revenge, from the 1736 edition of *The General History of the Pyrates.* Public domain.

Image 37
Page 152: Islamic galleon 1766, courtesy of the Metropolitan Museum of Modern Art, Accession number 2003.241 (2).

Image 38
Page 165: Paper cut out of men on the march by Richard Hall, c. 1780. Author's private collection.

Index